Strong Fathers Raise Strong Daughters

How to Raise a Confident, Emotionally Secure, and Empowered Daughter by Showing Up Every Day

Chloe Vaughn

Copyright © 2025 Chloe Vaughn. All rights reserved.

No part of this book may be reproduced, stored in a retrieval system, or transmitted in any form or by any means, electronic, mechanical, photocopying, recording, or otherwise, without the prior written permission of the publisher, except in the case of brief quotations embodied in critical articles or reviews.

The content of this publication is intended for informational and educational purposes only. While every effort has been made to ensure the accuracy and reliability of the information presented, the author and publisher make no representations or warranties regarding the completeness, applicability, or accuracy of the content. This book is not intended to replace professional advice, diagnosis, or treatment. Readers are encouraged to seek the guidance of licensed professionals where appropriate.

By reading this book, the reader acknowledges and agrees that the author and publisher shall not be held liable or responsible for any loss, injury, or damage, direct or indirect, that may result from the use or misuse of the information contained herein. This includes, but is not limited to, emotional, psychological, financial, legal, or physical consequences.

All trademarks, product names, or brand names mentioned herein are the property of their respective owners and are used for identification purposes only. The inclusion of any third-party material, quotes, or references is done in good faith and is believed to be within the bounds of fair use and public domain.

The reader assumes full responsibility for the application of any information provided in this book. Use of this publication signifies acceptance of these terms.

Contents

Introduction	1
1. You Are Her Hero	4
2. The Unique Power of Fatherhood	15
3. Connection in Early Childhood	27
4. Be Her Strength in Adolescence	38
5. Lead By Example	50
6. Risk Leads to Strength	63
7. Raising a Daughter Who Speaks Up	73
8. Physical Strength and Protection	83
9. Teach Her Real Love	93
10. Raising a Daughter of Character	108
11. Teach Your Daughter About Sex and Consent	123
Conclusion	128
References	130

Introduction

Growing up, I was lucky. I didn't wonder if my father loved me; I knew it. He always told me he loved me and how important I was to him, but it was more than that. I felt it in the way he looked at me when I accomplished something, even something small. I heard it in his voice when he told me he was proud. I saw it in the way he showed up; at school plays, my gymnastics class, my field hockey games, our late-night talks, and just ordinary days. It wasn't just the big moments that made an impact. It was his presence in the small, everyday things; the rides to school, the help with homework, the way he listened when I talked about nothing and everything. He hung out with me. I felt that he genuinely wanted to spend time with me. Those ordinary, mundane moments mattered. They built my sense of worth and cemented my belief that I was loved, that I mattered, and that I was deserving of love.

When you're a child, your world is small. It revolves around your home, your parents, and your everyday environment. And in that small world, a father holds tremendous power. A dad who is present and engaged doesn't just influence his daughter's day; he helps shape her entire sense of self. He teaches her, often without realizing it, that she is valuable, worthy of attention, and deserving of respect. His presence becomes the foundation of her confidence and emotional security.

But the opposite is also true. A father who is emotionally or physically absent leaves a void that can echo for years. A daughter who grows up without her father's presence may internalize a message that she is not enough to be chosen, prioritized, or deeply loved. That absence, whether it's through neglect, inconsistency, or distance, can quietly influence how she views herself, how she lets others treat her, and what she believes she's capable of.

The role a father plays in his daughter's life sets off a cascade of effects. It influences how she forms relationships, how she handles failure, how she dreams, and how she sees her place in the world. One of the most lasting impacts is in how she learns to relate to men. Her relationship with her father becomes the template, consciously or unconsciously, for how she will approach romantic partnerships, professional dynamics, and even friendships with men. A father who is loving, respectful, and consistent teaches his daughter what it feels like to be valued. As she grows, she will be far more likely to seek out and expect that same respect from others. She'll be prepared to recognize a healthy relationship when she sees one, and more importantly, to walk away from those that don't serve her well. By raising a securely attached daughter, a father sets her up to model emotional strength, self-respect, and healthy boundaries in every area of her life. The good news is that this kind of impact doesn't require perfection. It simply requires presence and consistency.

That's why I wrote this book.

Fathers can raise strong, confident, emotionally secure daughters, but they have to show up not just on holidays or significant milestones, but in the daily rhythm of life. You don't need to have all the answers.

You don't have to get everything right. But you do have to be there; consistently, attentively, and with intention.

This book is here to help you do that. It's for biological dads, stepdads, adoptive dads, single dads, co-parents, grandfathers, and mentors; any man who loves and supports a growing girl. Inside these pages, you'll find tools, background information, strategies, and relatable stories that you can use right away. Whether your daughter is a toddler, a teen, or a young adult, there is something here for you.

If you're reading this and feeling guilty about missed moments or fear that it's too late to make a difference, let me reassure you: it's not. Even small shifts can make a lasting impact. Your consistent presence, your willingness to try, and your commitment to connection will mean more to your daughter than you may ever fully realize.

By the end of this book, you'll understand just how influential your role is and how to use that power to help your daughter grow into the confident, emotionally secure, and empowered woman she was meant to be.

Remember, your daughter doesn't need you to be perfect.

She just needs you to be there.

Chapter One

You Are Her Hero

She may not always say it. She may roll her eyes, brush you off, or keep her headphones in while you talk. But do not be fooled. Your presence matters more than you know. You are not just part of her life; you are shaping it in ways that reach far beyond what is visible. From the earliest moments of her childhood to the turning points of adolescence, your daughter is watching, listening, and absorbing. The way you show up becomes her blueprint for what love feels like, what respect looks like, and how she deserves to be treated. To her, you are her first mirror. Through your eyes, she learns who she is and what she is worth. Whether you are fully confident in your parenting or still finding your footing, the truth remains the same: you are one of the most powerful influences in your daughter's life. She may not always express it, and you may not always feel it, but your words matter, your attention matters, and your presence matters.

What Being Her Hero Means

You do not need to be perfect. You do not need to have all the right answers. You just need to be there.

Being her hero is not about fixing every problem or offering constant praise. It is not about grand gestures. It is about the quiet, steady presence that tells her she is safe, that she is seen, and that she is loved. It is how you show up on the ordinary days that makes the biggest difference.

Consider the way she looks at you when you cheer her on from the sidelines. Think about how she leans into your voice during story time, or how her body relaxes when you put your arm around her after a hard day. These may seem like small things, but they are not. These are emotional deposits, investments in her sense of worth, that build her internal foundation and will support her for years to come.

You are the one who tells her, through your actions and your words, that she matters. You teach her what love feels like in its healthiest form: steady, respectful, and reliable. You model how to treat others, how to handle stress, and how to show compassion, even in moments of frustration. She is learning from you every day, even when you are not aware of it.

She watches how you treat the server at the restaurant. She notices how you speak to her mother, how you manage conflict, and whether you keep your promises. She may not be able to articulate it, but she is storing every interaction as a guide for what to expect from the world and from the people she will one day allow into her heart.

You are her first example of what a man can be. That is not something to fear; it is something to embrace. You are the first one who gets to show her what strength looks like when it is kind, what power looks like when it is gentle, and what love looks like when it is consistent.

Even when you make mistakes, and you will, your willingness to admit fault and try again teaches her something invaluable. She learns that real men do not hide from responsibility, that love is not about perfection but presence, and that people who care will always come back to do the work. That lesson alone can change the trajectory of her life.

You are the one who steadies her when the world gets loud, who believes in her before she knows how to believe in herself. You show up when it counts, and even more importantly, you show up when no one else is watching. That quiet consistency is the armor she will carry with her. It is the inner voice that will remind her she is never truly alone.

When she thinks about safety, she will think of you. When she thinks about what it feels like to be valued, protected, and heard, she will remember the way you made space for her, whether it was five minutes before bedtime or standing in line at the grocery store. She will remember that she mattered to you, and that will matter to her for the rest of her life.

The Research is Clear: Fathers Matter Deeply

For decades, we have known instinctively that a father's presence matters. But now, the research confirms it beyond a doubt. Study after study has shown that children with involved fathers are more likely to thrive socially, emotionally, and academically. For daughters specifically, the role of a loving and attentive father has a lifelong impact.

According to data published by the American Psychological Association, daughters who grow up with supportive and engaged fathers tend to have higher self-esteem, perform better in school, and are more likely to develop healthy boundaries in their relationships. They are also less likely to experience depression, eating disorders, or body image issues. A father's consistent presence shapes how a daughter sees herself and how she believes others should treat her.

Dr. Linda Nielsen, a professor at Wake Forest University and one of the leading experts on father–daughter relationships, writes that a daughter's sense of worth, confidence, and emotional security is often rooted in the quality of her relationship with her father. She emphasizes that fathers are not just nice to have; they are essential. Daughters who have strong, emotionally close bonds with their fathers tend to form stronger romantic partnerships in adulthood, have better stress-management skills, and are more resilient in the face of challenges.

Further, brain imaging studies have found that paternal involvement can actually influence the development of a child's prefrontal cortex, the part of the brain responsible for decision-making, emotional regulation, and impulse control. When fathers are actively engaged, they help wire their daughter's brain for long-term success.

And it is not just about being physically present. It is about emotional presence; being attuned, available, and responsive. When fathers validate their daughter's feelings, listen without judgment, and encourage her efforts, she learn to trust herself. She becomes more likely to advocate for herself, to pursue her goals, and to walk away from relationships that do not honor her worth.

The inverse is also true. When a father is distant, dismissive, or absent, a daughter is more likely to struggle with self-worth, seek external validation, and doubt her inner voice. These wounds can echo into adulthood, shaping how she sees herself and what she believes she deserves.

Fathers also play a unique role in helping their daughters develop independence and risk tolerance. While mothers are more likely to emphasize nurturing and safety, research shows that fathers often encourage exploration, challenge, and resilience. This balance between protection and empowerment is powerful. When a daughter hears her father say, "I believe in you," or watches him stand by her as she tries something difficult, it strengthens her belief in her own abilities. These experiences become internalized as grit and confidence, traits that serve her for a lifetime.

Moreover, fathers often influence how daughters perceive masculinity and relationships with men. A father who listens, respects boundaries, and models emotional regulation helps his daughter understand that strength and kindness are not opposites. She is less likely to confuse control with care or mistake possessiveness for love. Instead, she seeks partners who reflect the emotional integrity she has already experienced. In this way, fathers are not just shaping their daughters' childhoods; they are shaping their futures.

But when a father shows up consistently, lovingly, and wholeheartedly, he changes everything. He becomes the voice in her head that says, "You can do this," when life feels overwhelming. He becomes the standard she measures love against, the steady presence that reminds her she is worthy of being protected, supported, and deeply loved.

This is not about being perfect. The science does not demand perfection, only presence. What matters most is the quality of your connection. Even small, daily moments, such as sharing a meal, laughing at a joke, or asking her how her day went, can have a lasting impact. These interactions form the emotional scaffolding that helps her feel grounded and secure.

Fathers matter. Not just in theory, not just emotionally, but biologically, developmentally, and psychologically. Your presence is not optional; it is transformational. And your investment in your daughter's life will pay dividends far beyond what you may ever see.

Heroic Moments Look Ordinary

The most heroic things you do as a father will rarely feel heroic in the moment. They will not come with applause, dramatic music, or spotlight recognition. In fact, many of your greatest contributions to your daughter's life will happen quietly, almost invisibly, during the most ordinary days.

It is the way you look up from your phone when she walks in the room and give her your full attention. It is sitting beside her while she does her homework, not to correct every answer, but just to be near. It is making her breakfast before school, even if it is the same cereal every day. These small acts may seem unremarkable, but they carry deep meaning. They say, without words, "You matter to me. I see you. I am here."

When she is young, the way you lift her into the air, tie her shoes, or tuck her in at night builds more than routine; it builds trust. It teaches her that she can rely on you, and that love is found in presence, not performance. These moments create emotional safety, and that safety becomes the soil in which her self-worth will grow.

As she gets older, your heroism may look like showing up to a school event when work is busy, or waiting in the car while she finishes practice, even though you are tired. It might look like staying calm when she tells you something hard, or holding your tongue when she pushes your buttons. In those moments, when it would be easier to withdraw or react in frustration, your restraint becomes a shield. She may not thank you now, but she will remember your steady presence later.

Heroic fatherhood is not about making everything perfect; it is about making her feel safe when everything is not. It is about anchoring her during storms you cannot stop. When you listen without rushing to solve, when you sit beside her through a heartbreak without trying to fix it, when you offer a quiet hug instead of a lecture, those are the moments that become part of her emotional core.

She may not always say much, but she notices everything. She sees when you put your phone down to ask how her day went. She watches how you respond when she gets something wrong, or when she is in a bad mood and does not quite know why. If you meet her with patience, you are not only helping her through that moment, you are teaching her how to treat herself with gentleness in the future.

There will be times when she pulls away, when she seems uninterested, or even cold. These are not signs that you are not needed. These are signs that she is growing and testing the waters of independence. But even in those moments, she is watching to see if you will still show up. Your quiet consistency tells her, "I am not going anywhere," and that message builds a kind of trust that words alone cannot provide.

And then there are the moments when you don't even know she is paying attention. The way you respond to someone who cuts you off in traffic. The tone you use when talking to a customer service rep. The respect you show to her mother, even if you are no longer together. These seemingly forgettable interactions are actually powerful lessons. They show her how strength and dignity can coexist. They teach her what it looks like to move through the world with self-respect and kindness.

To your daughter, heroism rarely looks dramatic. It looks like you sitting beside her in silence when she is upset. It looks like you asking about her day and giving her your full attention when she answers. It looks like you tucking a note into her backpack just to remind her you are proud. It looks like you standing up for her, even when she is not in the room, and taking her seriously, even when she is still very young.

These small actions, repeated over time, build her confidence, create emotional safety, and help her understand what it means to be loved. She will remember the way you looked at her when she entered a room. She will carry the feeling of comfort you offered her when she needed it most. She will reflect the kindness and strength you modeled when she begins to form her own relationships.

The Hero She Will Never Forget

Years from now, she may not recall every gift you gave, every vacation you planned, or every piece of advice you offered. But she will remember that you were there. She will remember that you believed in her. She will remember that your love was never tied to her performance or achievements. She will remember that your arms were always a safe place to land.

This is what heroes do. And this is what you are becoming, one steady, intentional day at a time. So keep showing up. Keep listening, even when she pushes you away. Keep encouraging, even when she pretends not to care. Keep choosing love, especially when things feel difficult.

You are not just raising a daughter. You are shaping a future woman who will carry your words, your example, and your love with her for the rest of her life. And to her, you will always be the first man who made her feel like she was enough. Strong women are not born that way. They are raised by strong fathers who show up, who stay, and who make it clear that their daughters matter. You are her hero.

What She Needs Most Is You

What your daughter needs most is not perfection. She does not need you to be a mind reader, a millionaire, or a flawless role model. She does not need elaborate plans, endless entertainment, the latest fashion ry, or constant praise. What she needs most, what will shape her more than any lecture, lesson, or gift, is you. Fully present. Emotionally available. Steady, even when life is not.

When she looks to you, she is not just seeking approval; she is looking for a sense of grounding. In a world that often pulls her in a hundred directions, overwhelms her with images, and tells her who she should be, your steady presence offers a kind of emotional shelter. She may not say it out loud, but she feels it when you sit beside her without rushing, when you give her your full attention, when you ask how she is doing, and wait long enough to really hear the answer. Those are the moments when she knows she matters.

Children, and daughters especially, do not always articulate what they need in words. Their needs are evident in their behavior, tone, and silence. They appear when she lingers nearby, even when she claims she is fine. They show up when she asks to show you something, even if she acts like it's no big deal. When you respond with interest, patience, and presence, you give her something much more valuable than advice; you give her validation.

You do not need to fix every problem. In fact, sometimes the most meaningful thing you can do is let her speak without jumping in. Let her cry without rushing to make her stop. Let her be angry or confused without taking it personally. Your calm presence tells her, "You do not have to be okay for me to stay." That message will become part of her internal foundation. It will teach her that she is safe to be fully human: emotional, imperfect, and still worthy of love.

You are her safe place, and that does not require perfection. It requires consistency. Being there when you say you will. Following through on promises, no matter how small. Making time when it would be easier to opt out. These are the acts of strength that build her security. She learns that she can count on you. That when the world feels uncertain, her father is not.

Even as she grows more independent, do not mistake her self-sufficiency for not needing you. Adolescence will bring distance, and that is developmentally appropriate. She may begin to pull away, challenge your ideas, or act indifferent. But underneath all of it, she still needs the same thing, your steadiness. Your belief in her. Your presence, even in silence.

She may test your patience. She may close her door, roll her eyes, and shrug off your concern. Still, show up. Knock on her door anyway. Ask how she is doing, even if the answer is short. Invite her to dinner, even when she turns you down. These small, persistent gestures matter more than they seem. They tell her, over and over again, "You are worth showing up for."

What she needs most is not more stuff; it is connection. She needs a father who looks her in the eye when she speaks. Who does not just ask how school was, but listens when she says, "It was hard today." She needs to know that you are proud of her, not just for what she accomplishes, but for who she is. When she sees that your love does not depend on grades, trophies, or achievements, she learns that her worth is not something she has to earn.

She also needs to know that you see her, not just as your little girl, but as a whole person, complex, growing, and capable. When you listen to her ideas, ask for her opinion, and take her seriously, you help her trust her own voice. That self-trust will become one of her greatest assets. It will help her stand tall in rooms that try to make her small. It will give her the courage to speak up, to walk away from people who do not respect her, and to believe that her boundaries are valid and worth respecting.

The best way to help her become strong is to be strong for her, not controlling, not overbearing, but grounded and dependable. Your strength does not need to be loud or forceful. It shows up in your patience, your willingness to apologize, and your choice to stay calm when emotions rise. She watches you more closely than you realize. She is learning what strength looks like by how you carry yourself in everyday life.

Be the one who stays steady when things get hard. Be the one who listens when she feels unheard. Be the one who reminds her, by example, that love is not earned through perfection; it is given freely and consistently. Your presence in her life becomes the foundation she relies upon when she is unsure of which way to go. Your steadiness becomes the mirror that helps her recognize her own value.

This is the kind of fathering that does not always feel dramatic or grand. It may not seem extraordinary to you. But to her, it is everything. These quiet acts of emotional availability are not background noise; they are the soundtrack to her growing up feeling seen, safe, and loved.

And in doing this, you are not just helping her survive childhood or adolescence, you are preparing her for life. You are showing her how to love and how to be loved. You are teaching her that emotional safety is non-negotiable. You are shaping the kind of woman who knows her worth and does not settle for less.

Because in the end, the strength she will carry into the world is drawn from the strength you show her now. Not just in the big moments, but in all the ordinary ones. By being a strong father, emotionally grounded, present, patient, and reliable, you are raising a strong daughter. The kind of daughter who knows she is enough, because you never made her feel like she had to prove it.

Chapter Two

The Unique Power of Fatherhood

Fathers, let me say this very clearly: you are very important to your daughters, very important. The role you choose to play in your daughter's life will have an enormous impact on her sense of self. Your presence matters, perhaps more than you realize. Fathers possess a unique power to shape their daughters' self-confidence, their emotional security, and the choices they make for years to come. This power is not about grand gestures, big moments, or perfect words. It is rooted in small, daily actions and consistent care; a steady presence that creates confidence and resilience in a girl's life.

The Science Behind the Father-Daughter Bond

The connection between a father and daughter rests in both emotion, biology, and psychology. Modern research in child development and neuroscience underscores how pivotal your role is from the earliest days of your daughter's life. Longitudinal studies have followed girls from infancy into adulthood, revealing a pattern: daughters with involved fathers exhibit higher self-esteem and achieve more academically than those without this support. The presence of a father shapes a girl's belief in her abilities. She tends to approach challenges with confidence and is less likely to second-guess herself when she knows her dad believes in her.

Psychological research on attachment theory explains why this bond is so influential. When fathers engage positively, reading stories, listening attentively, and providing gentle guidance, they help their daughters develop emotional regulation skills. Girls learn how to handle disappointment, frustration, and even failure without losing hope. These emotional muscles grow strong through repeated practice with a trusted adult. Studies show that girls with responsive fathers are less prone to risk-taking behaviors and show greater resilience when facing setbacks.

On a neurological level, advances in MRI technology have allowed scientists to observe how children's brains respond to early care. Research reveals that consistent fatherly involvement promotes healthy brain development, especially in areas related to empathy, impulse control, and stress regulation. Daughters who experience warm, predictable interactions with their fathers display more robust neural connections in these regions. This biological groundwork translates into emotional security, a sense that the world is safe, relationships are trustworthy, and problems can be solved with support.

The difference between engaged and absent fathers is striking. Girls who grow up without reliable paternal support face higher rates of anxiety, depression, and substance abuse. Their academic performance may falter; they may struggle to form healthy bonds with peers or romantic partners later in life. Conversely, daughters who experience positive father involvement tend to delay sexual activity, choose healthier relationships, and demonstrate better decision-making as adults. None of this should inspire shame; it highlights the tremendous opportunity you as a father have to effect change.

Real-world stories make these findings tangible. Consider one father who decided, despite exhaustion from work, to read his daughter a story each night. Their ritual started small, ten minutes before bed, but over time, he noticed her willingness to share about her day growing. By the end of the school year, her grades had improved, and her teacher remarked on her newfound confidence and participation in class discussions. This transformation was not magic; it was the result of steady, loving attention.

The science is clear: your everyday actions are powerful. From infancy onward, your presence helps shape the architecture of your daughter's mind and heart. You give her a foundation for self-worth and the confidence to face life's complexities. No matter the age of your daughter, if she is a young child, in elementary school, a teenager, or a young woman, you can make a difference. You can start right now, today. You don't need any special skills; just be patient, consistent, and show up for your daughter, each and every day, in some small way.

What Dads Provide That's Different from Moms

Fathers bring something distinct and irreplaceable to their daughters' lives. This difference is not about superiority or competition but about balance. While mothers often create nurturing, emotionally supportive environments, fathers tend to introduce experiences that foster independence and a willingness to try new things. Dads encourage daughters to stretch their limits, take calculated risks, and develop a sense of autonomy. This unique encouragement can take the form of letting a daughter climb higher on the playground, cheering her on when she tries out for a team, or supporting her as she faces academic or social challenges. Through these moments, a daughter learns that setbacks are not disasters but opportunities to learn and grow. Fathers show their daughters, through both words and actions, that failure is not something to fear, but a bridge toward resilience.

The way fathers play and communicate with their daughters often nurtures a different set of strengths. Research shows that dads are more likely to engage in physical play, challenge games, or problem-solving activities. Rough-and-tumble play, a wrestling match on the living room floor, or a race in the backyard, teaches girls about boundaries, self-control, and how to manage strong emotions within safe limits. This style of interaction strengthens not just muscles but decision-making skills and confidence. When a father lets his daughter lead the way in a new activity or lets her "win" a friendly challenge, he is telling her she is capable and trustworthy. These experiences build self-assurance that extends far beyond childhood games.

Communication patterns differ as well. Dr. Linda Nielsen's research highlights how fathers tend to use more direct, concise language, making it critical for daughters to express themselves clearly and assertively in response. This regular practice gives girls the confidence to speak up, negotiate, and advocate for themselves in diverse environments, from classrooms to future workplaces. When fathers encourage their daughters to voice their opinions at the dinner table or discuss difficult topics without interruption, they are modeling respect for their perspective. Over time, this validation cultivates a strong sense of self-worth. Daughters learn they are worthy of being heard.

The influence of fathers reaches into areas of assertiveness and independence that are difficult to replicate in other relationships. Paternal affirmation, expressing pride in achievements, encouraging new ambitions, or simply listening with genuine interest, teaches girls they deserve to pursue their goals without apology. Fathers also tend to push boundaries differently than mothers. A dad might urge his daughter to try out for the debate team even if she is nervous, or suggest she stand up for herself when faced with unfair treatment by friends or teachers. These moments of gentle pressure help her discover internal strength she may not have realized existed.

Daughters also watch how their fathers interact with others, especially women, and internalize these lessons. The way a father treats his spouse, colleagues, or strangers becomes a blueprint for how his daughter expects to be treated in relationships later in life. When a father models respect, empathy, and fairness, he sets the stage for his daughter's future relationships with men and shapes her understanding of healthy boundaries and mutual respect. Dr. Nielsen's findings reveal that strong father-daughter communication can positively influence a girl's expectations for partnership, leadership roles, and even her willingness to negotiate salary or take on challenging projects as an adult.

Distinct behavioral patterns also reveal themselves in daily routines and boundary-setting. Fathers are more likely to set rules around independence, like curfews or responsibilities, while also providing flexibility for negotiation. This combination of structure and empowerment allows daughters to practice decision-making within safe boundaries. For example, when a dad allows his daughter to decide how she spends her free time while holding her accountable for schoolwork or chores, she learns both autonomy and responsibility.

A simple but powerful difference lies in the encouragement of exploration, whether it is introducing a new sport, traveling to unfamiliar places, or supporting creative pursuits. Fathers often push daughters beyond their comfort zones through these shared adventures. They give implicit permission to be bold and adventurous without losing sight of safety or respect.

If you're looking for a place to start, consider creating a simple tradition. Set aside one day a week as your "try something new" day. Let your daughter pick an activity, a topic, or a hobby she's curious about, and do it together. Whether it's a nature walk, learning a dance, watching a movie, or playing a game, engage with her. What matters is your attention and willingness to be present. She may decline sometimes, especially in the teen years, but don't worry, just keep at it. Your consistency sends a message: I care, and I'm here. The goal isn't perfection, but participation. Over time, these shared experiences build a lasting sense of value, connection, and self-worth. Remember, it's all about putting forth an intentional effort.

Fatherhood in Modern, Diverse Families

For too long, the idea of a strong father-daughter bond has been tied to the image of a traditional, two-parent family. This belief leaves many fathers and daughters feeling as if a meaningful connection is out of reach for them. In reality, families today come in many forms, such as single-parent households, blended families, and homes shaped by diverse cultural backgrounds. What matters most is not whether a home fits a certain mold, but whether fathers or father figures show up with intention, reliability, and care. The "father effect" crosses boundaries of biology, geography, and marital status. It does not depend on living under the same roof or sharing the same blood. Instead, it grows out of daily effort and emotional openness.

Many still hold the misconception that only biological fathers can foster these deep bonds or that stepfathers and other father figures are somehow secondary. However, evidence shows that stepfathers who invest in shared activities, like having a tea party together, reading books together, or going on bike rides, can form attachments that are equally strong and meaningful. One stepfather I know connected to his teenage stepdaughter over their mutual love of astronomy. Together, they charted constellations from the backyard, transforming awkward silences into laughter and trust. Their connection did not spring from genetics but from shared wonder and consistent presence.

Distance poses another challenge that is often misunderstood. Some believe that if a father does not live with his daughter, closeness cannot be achieved. However, fathers separated by miles, due to work, divorce, or military service, have shown remarkable creativity in staying connected. A long-distance dad I met set up a daily ritual of Zoom calls with his daughter before bedtime. Even when he was in a different country, she knew he would ask about her day and listen to her stories. Over time, their conversations became a touchstone she relied on for reassurance and encouragement. Technology has become a bridge rather than a barrier for many families striving to maintain bonds across distance.

Cultural diversity brings unique traditions and expectations around fatherhood, but the core need for reliable adult support remains unchanged. In some cultures, extended family members step into fatherly roles when needed; in others, fathers find ways to support their daughters' aspirations even when community norms differ from mainstream expectations. Research now recognizes that the impact of an involved father figure is just as powerful in these varied settings.

Daughters benefit from encouragement, protection, and modeling, regardless of the exact family structure.

The myth that only "standard" families can cultivate strong father-daughter relationships has left many feeling excluded or invisible in mainstream parenting advice. You may have encountered books or articles that presume every father tucks his daughter in at night or attends every school event in person. This narrow lens misses the reality faced by millions of families who build closeness through text messages, weekend visits, or simple acts of remembering important dates. The truth is that what shapes a daughter's confidence and emotional security is not who her father is on paper but how he shows up in her real life; by listening deeply, celebrating milestones (even virtually), and never letting physical distance become emotional absence.

A growing body of research has finally caught up with this reality. Studies now include data on stepfamilies, single-parent households, and multicultural homes. They find that girls with any consistently supportive male adult, stepfather, grandfather, uncle, or mentor, are more likely to thrive academically and emotionally than those without such figures. The act of showing up matters more than any title or living arrangement.

Why It's Never Too Late to Start Making a Difference

Many fathers worry that lost years or past mistakes make it impossible to build meaningful relationships with their daughters. Regret over missed birthdays, school events, and everyday rituals often lingers, especially after years of distraction, work, or family upheaval. Yet, this belief does not align with what science or experience shows: the heart and brain are capable of change at any age. Research on neuroplasticity, the brain's ability to form new connections well into adulthood, demonstrates that people can reshape relationships and emotional habits long after childhood. Even where wounds and patterns of distance exist, fathers and daughters can develop new ways of relating that create trust, security, and affection.

Adolescents and adults alike have the neural flexibility to build healthier attachment patterns when offered consistent care and emotional presence. Studies confirm that, with time and patience, it is possible to recover from relational injuries and create strong, supportive bonds later in life. Every positive interaction, no matter how small, strengthens the network of trust between father and daughter. This process requires intention and effort, but not perfection. Despite time lost or lingering pain, repair is always possible.

Re-engaging is about more than simply being present; it requires humility and honest acknowledgment of the past. A sincere apology holds significant power. Fathers sometimes fear that admitting faults will undermine their position, but the opposite is true; it builds credibility and paves the way for healing. When apologizing, be specific: instead of general regret, say, "I know I missed important moments in your life, and I am truly sorry for the hurt that I caused." Don't rush forgiveness or expect quick results; give your daughter space to process. Sometimes writing a letter first helps to clarify your thoughts and ease the initial anxiety for both of you.

After apologizing, focus on rebuilding gradually through consistent actions: small, reliable rituals like weekly calls, occasional outings, or regular text messages about daily events. If the relationship feels fragile, start with low-pressure interactions: going out to a movie, a walk in the park, or simply some shared time with no set agenda. Let your daughter steer the conversation and choose activities; this demonstrates respect for her boundaries and interests.

A phased trust-building plan can ease the way forward. Start with brief, regular contact, perhaps a daily text. Slowly increase the frequency and depth of interactions as trust grows. Celebrate small milestones, but don't demand more than your daughter is ready to give. When setbacks arise, respond patiently; rebuilding often follows a non-linear path.

Here is a template for a heartfelt apology many fathers find effective: *I know I haven't always been there in the way you needed or deserved. Looking back, I see places where I let you down or made choices that hurt you. I am deeply sorry for those times. If you're willing, I want to start again, not to erase the past, but to build something better going forward. I want to listen more and be part of your life in ways that matter to you.* And then you need to wait and let your daughter process. It may take time, don't get upset about that. Give her that time. Continue to gently remind her that you are here and hoping for a better future with her, and look forward to spending time with her.

One father I know thought it was too late to reconnect with his adult daughter after years of silence post-divorce. Encouraged to reach out, he wrote a letter, recognizing her pain and making no demands. Weeks later, she replied with a tentative text. Gradually, their exchanges grew into regular conversations, shared holidays, and laughter over old and new memories. Today, their bond centers on present honesty and warmth. took patience and time, but they got there.

Guilt often traps fathers in cycles of regret. The challenge is to move beyond guilt and take purposeful steps forward. Each day offers a fresh chance to rewrite stories with new choices. Regardless of your daughter's age, what matters is what you do now: offering attention, humility, consistency, and hope for renewal. The past shapes us, but does not define our future as fathers or families.

The Ripple Effect: How Dad's Actions Shape a Daughter's Future

Even the smallest moments can leave lasting imprints. A father practicing his daughter's dance routine with her, asking thoughtful questions, or showing up consistently sends a message: You matter. You are worthy of my time and undivided attention. That message becomes part of a daughter's inner voice.

Research continues to reveal how these everyday interactions form the building blocks of future success. Studies tracking girls from childhood into adulthood have found clear links between early paternal encouragement and women's pursuit of leadership positions later in life. Daughters who recall their fathers encouraging their curiosity, applauding their efforts, and supporting their ambitions are more likely to seek out competitive fields, speak their minds in professional settings, and persist through setback. The encouragement and care a girl receives from her father in childhood stay with her, becoming a lasting part of who she is as a woman

Consider another scenario: a teenage girl sits at the kitchen table, anxious about an upcoming exam. Her father sets aside his phone, asks her about her worries, and helps her break down the challenges into manageable steps. He reassures her that mistakes are only part of learning. Even if she falters this time, she knows he will help her try again. Years later, when faced with obstacles at work or in relationships, she draws on that memory, not just of solving algebra, but of learning that setbacks do not define her worth or limit her future. She develops grit, not because life was easy, but because someone taught her how to get through difficulties without losing faith in herself.

Fatherly affection and validation also serve as powerful shields against unhealthy relationships. Data shows that daughters who experience warm, consistent affirmation from their fathers are less susceptible to seeking approval from partners at the cost of their own well-being. Instead, they recognize their value and set boundaries with greater confidence. These women tend to resist toxic dynamics and choose partners who respect them, reflecting the self-respect fostered years earlier by an attentive parent.

The ripple effect extends into mental health as well. Regular positive engagement, such as shared meals, listening without judgment, or simply expressing pride, lowers the risk of depression and anxiety in young women. These moments communicate that her feelings matter and that she is never alone with her struggles. Over time, this emotional scaffolding allows her to reach out for help when needed and develop healthy coping mechanisms as life grows more complex.

Even routine acts can echo through a lifetime. Picture a father who always asks his daughter about her favorite book or encourages her to teach him a new skill. These exchanges might seem small, a few minutes before bedtime or chatter during errands, but they signal respect for her individuality. She learns that her ideas hold value and that her interests are worth sharing. This validation strengthens her voice and gives her permission to pursue her passions without apology.

Here is a great and easy way to start showing your daughter she has value and you are interested in her likes, hobbies, and interests. Ask your daughter to talk to you about or show you something she's passionate about, and then just listen. Let her know you value what she cares about, what she enjoys, and who she is becoming.

These small actions may not seem like much in the moment, but their consistency leaves a lasting mark, helping your daughter grow into a strong, confident, and emotionally secure woman.

Chapter Three

Connection in Early Childhood

From birth to age five, a child's brain develops more rapidly than at any other time in life, forming the emotional and neurological wiring that will shape how she learns, connects, and trusts. Studies show that consistent, loving interactions with caregivers, especially fathers, support secure attachment, increase emotional resilience, and lay the foundation for healthy self-esteem. These early years offer a powerful window to build that connection, one moment at a time.

Making Moments Count: Connection Through Everyday Routines

Early childhood is a time when routines quietly shape your daughter's sense of safety, love, and belonging. In those early years, it's the simple, repeated moments that matter most: bedtime stories, shared meals, quiet conversations before sleep. These ordinary rhythms of daily life may seem insignificant, but they are not; they are powerful chances to build connection and trust. Reading your daughter a bedtime story may seem like a small thing, but to her, it's everything. As you sit beside her with a familiar book in your hands, your voice becomes part of her sense of comfort and safety. She may not remember the details of the story years from now, but she will remember *you,* being there, night after night. These moments tell her that she matters, that she's worth your time, and that she's never alone. Your steady presence during these simple routines becomes something she can count on, shaping her sense of security, her confidence, and the way she comes to see herself in the world.

Children thrive on repetition. A nightly routine, whether it involves reading a beloved story or inventing a new one, becomes more than a way to wind down; it is a signal that the world is consistent and stable. When you add silly voices or let your daughter become a character in the story, you invite laughter and participation, turning a simple bedtime into a cherished ritual she will remember long after the details fade. You could sing a special lullaby together or create a personalized song. These personal touches become embedded into her sense of security. She learns that this time is sacred and that her father's presence is dependable.

Mundane tasks provide opportunities for connection if you approach them with intention. Bath time, often hurried or overlooked, can transform into a playful sanctuary. Turn washing her hair into a gentle game; try having "bubble beard contests" or let her play with her favorite bath toys as you share stories about your own childhood baths. Through these moments, she sees that you care and are interested in her, and she feels valued. Ask her about her favorite part of the day while you rinse the shampoo. Your engagement signals that you are not just there to supervise, but to share the experience.

Children crave consistency, and predictable routines help them feel anchored when the world feels big or uncertain. The repetition of nightly rituals, such as brushing your teeth together, reading a story, or sharing the best and worst part of your day, teaches her that even as she grows and changes, some things remain constant. Most importantly, it teaches her that her father's love is constant. At some point in the evening, try asking her to name three things she loved about today. This will teach her that her experiences and feelings are meaningful and matter.

Being present isn't about the amount of time; it means being fully engaged in the moment. Even brief, focused moments can build meaningful connections. If your schedule is tight, look for small windows to create simple routines that can be easily sustained. A five-minute song or a short story before bed can help ease her worries and send her to sleep feeling loved and secure. A secret handshake or a special goodbye wave in the morning can turn a rushed moment into one that feels personal and important. These small acts show her that she matters and that she's always on your mind.

When work or responsibilities pull you away, try simple ways to stay connected. Record yourself reading her favorite story so she can hear your voice when you're not there. Leave a quick note under her pillow with a doodle or message for her to find at bedtime. If mornings are hectic, create a fun, consistent ritual, such as a superhero pose in the hallway or a whispered "go conquer the day" just between the two of you. These small gestures take little time but go a long way in keeping your bond strong.

Creating Emotional Safety Through Secure Attachment

From the earliest moments of her life, your daughter turns to you for comfort, protection, and reassurance. This instinct is rooted in secure attachment, the emotional bond between parent and child that forms the basis for how she will trust, connect, and relate to others. When you consistently respond with warmth, empathy, and reliability, you help shape her brain for emotional strength and resilience. According to attachment theory, developed by John Bowlby and Mary Ainsworth, children who experience dependable care develop an internal sense of safety and approach the world with curiosity rather than fear. You don't need formal training to support this bond. What matters most is being present and responsive to her needs.

How you respond during emotionally charged moments plays a key role in building this trust. If she's overwhelmed, upset, or melting down after a long day, your presence and reaction can either soothe or intensify her distress. Instead of correcting or distracting her right away, kneel to her level and make eye contact. Let her see that you're fully there. Offer a hug or hold her hand if she wants comfort. If she can't express what she's feeling right away, simply staying close and calm is often enough to help her begin to regulate her emotions.

Staying grounded in those moments isn't always easy, especially when you are tired or frustrated. It's natural to feel impatient or tempted to walk away, but your ability to pause and regulate your own emotions models exactly what you want her to learn. Take a breath, acknowledge the difficulty, and name what's happening: "This is a hard moment for both of us." If she lashes out or cries uncontrollably, avoid punishment. Instead, help her find words: "You're upset that we had to leave the park. That makes sense. It's okay to feel that way." Validating her emotions teaches her that they're not wrong or shameful; they're a natural part of being human and worth understanding.

Creating emotional safety is shaped by your daily habits and how you handle challenging moments. Let her speak freely, knowing she won't be judged or punished for her words. When she admits to a mistake or shares something awkward or embarrassing, listen without rushing to correct or fix it. Your acceptance now lays the groundwork for open communication as she grows. You might also set aside a calming space at home, a cozy spot with soft pillows, books, or stuffed animals, where she knows she can go when she needs support. Let her know it's always there, just like you are.

The Power of Play: Confidence, Leadership, and Connection

Play is more than just fun; it's how your daughter learns to move through the world. Through play, she develops not only coordination and imagination but also problem-solving skills, emotional resilience, and social awareness. When you join her in the sandbox or dash around the playground, you're not just passing the time; you're showing her she matters. You're helping her build the confidence to take risks, adapt to change, and trust herself.

Imaginative games, like turning the jungle gym into a pirate ship or pretending the slide is a dragon's tail, fuel creativity and flexibility. Physical play, like climbing and swinging, strengthens her body and deepens her belief in her abilities. When she falls and gets back up, she learns that mistakes aren't failures, they're part of growing.

Your presence changes everything. Rather than watching from the sidelines or scrolling through your phone, step into her world. Be her co-adventurer. Let her lead the mission. When you follow her invented rules or join in a silly game, you're telling her, "Your ideas matter." This playful role reversal builds her agency and confidence; she sees herself as a leader, and she sees you respecting her voice.

Inviting her to explain the rules of tag or guide you through the latest game shows her she's capable. And when she senses your genuine interest, her self-esteem blooms.

These shared moments give you a window into how she handles setbacks, peer dynamics, and social dilemmas. When a child changes the rules or asks to join in, don't rush to intervene. Let her practice compromise and communication. If she feels uncertain or shy, your quiet presence, just a nod, a smile, or a gentle "I'm right here", can be enough for her to try again. And when she climbs higher than ever or bravely crosses a wobbly bridge, your encouragement becomes a voice she carries within: *I can do hard things.*

Play is also where she learns that challenges are meant to be faced, not feared. Age-appropriate risks, like trying new challenges or leading a game, help her reframe uncertainty as adventure. If she slips or hesitates, don't swoop in. Instead, say, "That was brave. Want to try again together?" These moments reinforce the value of effort over perfection and teach her to bounce back stronger.

Rituals can turn everyday playground visits into lasting memories. Creating playful traditions, like shouting a silly code word before takeoff on the swing, or pausing for a "power-up" dance before the big slide, gives your daughter emotional anchors. These small but meaningful gestures say, *"You're brave. I believe in you."* When she feels unsure or hesitant, these familiar rituals help her reset and face the moment with courage.

Over time, these shared habits become touchstones, proof that your bond goes beyond the usual routines of home life. They offer consistency and comfort, especially when she's venturing into something new or uncertain. Your rituals remind her that she's not alone; she has someone in her corner cheering her on.

Each playground visit is also a chance to model the values you want her to carry into the world. When you show patience while waiting for your turn or kindness to another child who's upset, she learns by watching. She sees that real strength includes empathy, fairness, and respect. These quiet lessons become her internal compass for building friendships, succeeding in school, and facing life's inevitable challenges.

As your daughter grows, her games will change, but her need for joyful connection will remain the same. Whether you're shooting hoops in the driveway, building a blanket fort, or racing to the mailbox, these moments keep your relationship playful and strong. The resilience, creativity, and confidence she develops through play won't stay on the playground. They'll grow with her because you showed up and were there, right beside her, playing too.

Supporting Her Through Big Emotions

You may notice that with toddlers, emotions run at full volume. The slightest disruption, a favorite block out of reach, or a sudden switch from play to bedtime can spark an outburst that feels disproportionate to the moment. These meltdowns are not signs of failure or defiance; they're simply evidence of a young brain learning how to handle frustration, disappointment, and transition. For fathers, anticipating the moments that trip these emotional wires is half the battle. Transitions, especially from something fun like playing to something less exciting like bedtime or leaving the playground, often become flashpoints. You can set yourself up for fewer battles by providing warnings before changes happen: a simple "five more minutes, then we clean up" gives her a sense of control and prepares her mind to shift gears.

Toddlers don't yet have the words to describe what's going on inside them. You play an important role in teaching emotional vocabulary and showing her how to manage those big feelings. One powerful tool is the use of "feelings cards", simple drawings or photos of faces showing different emotions. Sit down together and practice naming them: happy, sad, frustrated, excited, scared. When your daughter's face clouds with anger or tears well up, reach for those cards and ask her to point to the one that matches her feeling. This practice helps her turn confusion into understanding and see that all emotions have names and are normal. Deep breathing is another fundamental skill that can be taught as a game. Try the "smell the flower, blow out the candle" method, inhale slowly as if smelling a flower, then exhale as if blowing out a candle on a birthday cake. Do it together, side by side, so she sees you using the same tool she's learning to use.

When your daughter erupts in anger or sadness, it's easy to want to "fix" things or distract her from how she feels. Instead, begin with validation. Use simple, calm phrases that acknowledge her experience without judgment: "It's okay to feel mad. I'm here with you." Or say, "You look upset because playtime ended." These small statements let her know she's not alone and that you accept her emotions, even when they are big and messy. Avoid phrases like "Don't cry" or "You're fine." While well-intended, such words may teach her to suppress her feelings. Your goal is not to end the feelings quickly but to help her move through them safely.

Sometimes, despite your best efforts, emotions will overflow. In these moments, having a quick list of reset activities can make all the difference. Movement helps shift energy and refocus attention. Try suggesting jumping jacks or a "shake out the grumpies" dance together, get silly, wave your arms, and encourage laughter to break through tension. A silly face contest can also work wonders: challenge each other to make the most outrageous expression possible in the mirror. The act of switching gears from frustration to fun helps her body calm down while showing her that big feelings are temporary and manageable.

Physical and sensory strategies are particularly effective with young children because their brains respond strongly to touch and movement. If she seems overwhelmed, offer a firm but gentle squeeze of her hand or suggest squeezing a soft stuffed animal together. Sometimes, handing her a cold washcloth or asking her to find something soft to hug can redirect her attention from upset to comfort. These resets don't erase her emotions but give her space to recover without shame.

Your modeling in these moments is as important as any script or activity. When you show patience by taking a slow breath or using a gentle tone, even when you're frustrated, you teach self-regulation by example. If you lose your cool, own it: "I was frustrated too, but I'm taking deep breaths now." This honesty teaches her that everyone struggles at times, but there are ways to handle difficult moments without hurting anyone or shutting down.

Anticipating triggers, naming feelings, validating emotions, providing physical outlets, and modeling your own regulation lay a foundation for emotional intelligence that lasts far beyond toddlerhood. Through these strategies and habits, you help your daughter understand how to manage her own storms and that she will always have someone steady in her corner as she does.

Everyday Affirmations: Showing Love Without Words

Love between a father and daughter often shows up in small, consistent actions. A squeeze of her hand at drop-off, eye contact when she's talking, or a steady hug before school all send the message: *I care. I'm here.* When you kneel beside her and give her your full attention, she feels seen. A pat on the back, a nod of encouragement, or simply walking at her pace tells her she matters. These nonverbal gestures build a sense of safety and connection that doesn't depend on words.

Children notice the difference between distraction and genuine attention. When you make the effort to really listen, whether she's showing you a drawing or performing a dance routine, you're giving her more than approval. You're reinforcing her worth. Affection doesn't have to be dramatic. A high five after a small win, a quick ruffle of her hair, or holding her close at night creates a pattern of emotional support that stays with her.

Simple, creative routines can turn these affirmations into lasting habits. Leaving a note in her lunchbox, a doodle, a joke, or a short message lets her know she's on your mind. Drawing a heart on her hand before school gives her a quiet reminder that she's supported, even when you're apart. She may look at it during the day and remember your presence.

Setting aside time for routines adds another layer of stability. Maybe it's a Saturday morning breakfast at the same spot, always starting with a special handshake you two created. These shared customs matter, not for what they are, but because they show consistency. They remind her that your relationship is steady. Over time, these regular actions become part of how she understands love and reliability.

Repeated over time, these small gestures help shape how your daughter sees herself. When she encounters hard moments, disagreements with friends, pressure at school, or self-doubt, these memories help ground her. She remembers that she is cared for. Children who receive regular affirmations like these often approach life with greater confidence, handle setbacks with more ease, and show more empathy toward others.

You don't need elaborate plans or constant attention. What matters is being consistent and sincere. She may not remember every detail, but she will remember how you made her feel. The note in her lunch box, the heart on her palm, and a familiar routine at breakfast all tell her that she is valued. These steady actions add up.

As this chapter comes to a close, take a moment to reflect on how these small, everyday choices contribute to building a lasting foundation. They teach your daughter to trust not only in your relationship but also in herself. The affirmations and steady presence you offer now give her something solid to carry with her, through childhood and into adulthood. Strong fathers make strong daughters, and it's through your quiet consistency that her confidence, resilience, and sense of self-worth begin to take root. In the next chapter, we'll explore how to keep that connection strong as she steps further into her independence.

Chapter Four

Be Her Strength in Adolescence

The teen years can feel like she is pulling away, but this is when your presence matters most. This chapter shows how strong fathers stay steady, set boundaries, and keep showing up through the silence

Stand Steady Through the Storm

Something shifts during the teenage years. The daughter who once leapt into your arms now barely looks up from her phone. Her laughter at your jokes is replaced by silence or sarcasm. She spends more time in her room with her door shut, lost in the glow of a screen. She might seem glued to social media, earbuds in, eyes focused on a digital world that feels increasingly closed to you. And when you try to reach out, asking about her day, offering a ride, or suggesting spending time together, you are met with shrugs, short answers, or no response at all.

For many fathers, this change is heartbreaking. It can feel like rejection. But it is not. What you are seeing is a normal, age-appropriate development shift. She is beginning the process of separating, forming her own identity, and moving beyond childhood. That does not mean she no longer needs you. It means she needs you differently. The key is not to mistake distance for disconnection. Beneath the headphones, behind the sarcasm, is still your daughter, searching, struggling, and hoping you won't give up on her.

This period of separation is part of how she begins to see herself as an individual. Psychologists call it individuation, the process of learning who she is apart from you, her parents, and the safety of childhood. It is not easy for her either. One moment, she wants independence and freedom. The next, she craves reassurance and support. She may reject affection, pull away emotionally, and test your patience. But at her core, she is still looking to you for stability, approval, and strength. She is trying to figure out, "Am I okay?" And your presence answers that question more powerfully than anything else.

This is when you must become her anchor. The world she is stepping into is loud and fast. It is filled with pressure to be perfect, to fit in, to look a certain way, and to constantly be available online. Social media has amplified every adolescent insecurity. She may be comparing herself to filtered images that no one can live up to. She may feel anxious about missing out, excluded from a group chat, or crushed by a single negative comment. Her phone may seem like her lifeline, but it can also be a source of constant stress, emotional exhaustion, and even identity confusion.

That is why she needs you to set the boundaries she cannot yet set for herself. Your strength now means holding the line when it comes to screen time, family rules, and emotional well-being. You are not being overprotective; you are being responsible. Have clear, consistent expectations for when devices are put away: at meals, during family time, and before bed. Make your home a place where presence matters more than posts. She may roll her eyes or protest, but deep down, these boundaries give her a sense of safety. They tell her that someone cares enough to say, "This matters."

More importantly, check in with her. Ask how she is feeling; not just what happened in school, but how she is doing emotionally. Look for signs of overwhelm, such as changes in sleep, constant scrolling, withdrawal, irritability, or self-criticism. Ask open-ended questions, and then listen. You do not need to solve her problems. You only need to care, consistently and without judgment. Let her know you are paying attention, even if she pretends not to notice.

You might feel unsure about what to say. That is okay. You do not have to deliver the perfect speech or have all the answers. Just being present matters. Sit on the edge of her bed and ask if she wants a snack. Invite her to go for a drive or watch a show together. If she says no, try again later. Your steadiness and willingness to keep showing up build a foundation of trust. It teaches her that love is not conditional, and support does not vanish when things get hard.

Do not assume that because she is spending more time alone, she no longer wants a connection. What she often wants is space without pressure. Your presence, even in silence, tells her she is not alone. You do not need access to every thought in her head. You only need to be available when she's ready to talk. That trust takes time to build, and it grows through repetition. Your strength is not in forcing your way in. It is in being the one who never leaves.

This season of adolescence can feel like a storm: loud, chaotic, and unpredictable. But storms are not permanent. They pass. When she looks back on these years, she may not remember every word you said. But she will remember the way you stayed calm when she was spinning, the way you kept showing up, and the way your presence made her feel safe.

This is the core of what it means to be a strong father to a teenage daughter. Not to dominate or fix her, but to hold space, stay steady, and be the one constant she can count on. You are teaching her how to trust, how to stay grounded in chaos, and how to believe that she is never alone. Even when she seems distant, even when the silence stretches long, your strength is shaping the woman she is becoming.

Be the Standard: Set the Rules, Model the Values, Hold the Line

Teenagers are wired to test limits. It is part of how they develop independence, self-awareness, and confidence. But while your daughter may act like she wants complete freedom, she still needs structure. She may roll her eyes at your rules, argue over your expectations, and push back on your decisions, but deep down, she finds security in knowing that someone is paying attention to her. Rules are not signs of control or distrust. They are signs of love. And when they are consistent, fair, and rooted in values, they become one of the most important tools you have as a father.

Your daughter is watching you closely, even if she pretends not to be. She notices how you handle stress, how you speak to others, and how you deal with conflict. She hears what you say, but more importantly, she watches what you do. If you expect her to be kind, but you speak with sarcasm or impatience, she sees the gap. If you want her to manage screen time, but you are always glued to your phone, she feels the double standard. As a father, your influence is most powerful when your actions match your words. When your behavior aligns with your values, you teach her something she will carry for the rest of her life: integrity.

Being the standard does not mean being perfect. It means being consistent. If you say phones are off during dinner, then yours should be off too. If you expect her to show respect, you must show it in return, even when the conversation is hard. Boundaries are more than rules; they are opportunities to teach. When you hold the line with love, without yelling or guilt, you show her what it means to lead with strength and compassion.

It is common for fathers to fear that being firm will damage the relationship. However, the truth is that girls do not respect inconsistency. If the rules change based on your mood, if you give in to avoid an argument, or if you try to be more of a friend than a parent, she learns to push further, not trust deeper. She needs to know what to expect from you. Predictability builds safety. A daughter who knows what the limits are and why they exist feels grounded, even when she does not like the rules.

Family rules should reflect your core values. They are not about power, they are about protection. Set clear expectations around screen time, bedtime, school responsibilities, chores, and curfews. Make sure she understands the rules and why they matter. "We value honesty in this house," or "We keep phones out of bedrooms because sleep is important for your health," are simple statements that connect the rule to a principle. The more she understands the *why*, the more she will begin to internalize those values as her own.

Enforcing rules also means following through with consequences. When your daughter breaks a boundary, resist the urge to get angry or take it personally. Stay calm and direct. Explain the consequence, then hold to it. If you say she loses the car keys for the weekend, do not give them back early because she apologized. Empathy is important, but so is consistency. When she sees that your word means something, she learns to trust you and to take responsibility for her choices.

This is also the time to create space for conversations about values. Ask her what she thinks is right or wrong in situations she sees online, in movies, or among her peers. Talk about relationships, pressure, honesty, and reputation. These talks do not have to be long or forced.

Sometimes, a few thoughtful sentences during a car ride or while doing dishes are enough. What matters is that you are inviting her to think and reflect. You are not just managing her behavior—you are shaping her character.

One powerful way to reinforce values is through rituals. Make family meals a priority, even if they are short or simple. Use that time to check in, share stories, and talk about real things. Begin and end the day with a moment of connection: a quick hug, a shared prayer, or a few words of encouragement. These rituals create rhythm, and rhythm builds resilience. In a world that constantly pulls her in different directions, family rituals offer something solid she can return to.

There will be times when she disagrees with you, when she thinks your rules are unfair, or when she tests how serious you really are. Do not take these moments as threats to your authority. See them as chances to remind her who you are: a father who means what he says, who leads with love, and who holds steady even when things get tense. Your calm consistency does more than maintain order. It sends a deeper message: she is worth the effort. Her growth is worth the challenge.

Being the standard means being willing to lead, to correct, and to protect. It means holding the line when it is easier to give in. It means living out the values you want her to carry into adulthood. And it means trusting that even when she acts like she is not listening, she is absorbing everything.

When your daughter becomes a woman, she will face a world filled with choices, pressures, and competing messages. What you teach her now about rules, respect, and responsibility will become the foundation she uses to stay grounded. Be the standard. Hold the line. And know that every moment you lead with strength and love, you are building something far more lasting than compliance; you are building character.

Guard Her Circle: Stay Involved in Her World Without Invading It

As your daughter grows older, her world begins to widen. Friends become more important. Outside voices start to carry more weight. The things that influence her, such as the music she listens to, the shows she watches, and the conversations she has at school or online, start to shape how she sees herself and how she understands the world. This is part of her development, and it is necessary. But it also comes with real risks.

She is stepping into a world where peer pressure is relentless, where social media feeds often shape image and identity, and where fitting in can feel more important than being herself. She is trying to figure out who she is and where she belongs. In the middle of all this, she needs you, not as a shadow, not as a micromanager, but as a steady presence who knows her world well enough to step in when needed, and wise enough to give space when appropriate.

You do not need to know everything about her social life, but you do need to care enough to ask. Know the names of her friends. Ask what she likes about them, what they do when they spend time together, and what kind of conversations they have. These questions are not about control; they are about connection. They show her that her life matters to you and that you are paying attention. If she rolls her eyes or gives short answers, do not let that discourage you. Keep showing up in small ways, without prying. Your presence communicates something bigger than the words ever will.

Social media complicates this even further. The friendships your daughter has do not only exist at school or practice. They exist in DMs, group chats, video shares, and comment threads that unfold around the clock. The digital world does not sleep. And it does not care about her well-being. While there are positive aspects, such as connecting with peers, exploring interests, and discovering creativity, there are also darker corners: bullying, exclusion, comparison, and exposure to messages that can be harmful or misleading.

You cannot monitor everything. You should not try. But you *can* keep the door open for conversations about what is happening online. Ask questions like, "What apps are your friends into right now?" or "What kind of things do you see on TikTok or Instagram that make you laugh or think?" These questions do not feel like surveillance. They feel like interest. When you ask with curiosity instead of suspicion, she is more likely to answer.

Teach her to look out for red flags, when a friend starts gossiping, when someone pressures her to do something she is not comfortable with, when an online interaction feels off. Let her know that no matter what happens, she can always come to you for support. Say it clearly: "Even if you make a mistake, or something goes wrong, I will not be angry, I will help." This gives her the courage to tell you the truth when it matters most.

Some fathers worry about being too involved or stepping on their daughter's independence. But involvement is not the same as intrusion. You do not need to know every detail to be present. You do not need to approve of every friend to care about her well-being. It's okay to raise questions if you notice patterns, friends who consistently disregard boundaries, friendships that seem emotionally draining, or situations where she appears less like herself. Ask gently. Say, "You seem quiet after being with them, everything okay?" or "That doesn't sound like someone who treats you with a lot of respect." She may not respond right away, but she will remember that you noticed and cared.

Make your home a safe and welcoming place for her friends. If possible, let them hang out at your house. Keep snacks in the pantry, be friendly but not overbearing, and stay visible. When her friends know and respect you, they are less likely to cross lines. More importantly, it gives you a window into her world without forcing it open. You do not need to eavesdrop; you just need to be around.

The same goes for teachers, coaches, and other adults in her life. Know who they are. Attend events, show your face, shake hands, ask questions. Let your daughter see that you are not connected to the world she is part of. She may pretend she does not care, but your involvement shows that her life matters to you in a deeper way.

It is important, too, to model the kind of relationships you want her to pursue. How you treat your partner, your family, your friends, all of it is teaching her what is normal and acceptable. She is learning what to expect from others by watching what you allow, what you tolerate, and what you protect. She will carry those lessons into her own friendships and future relationships.

As a father, you are not meant to eliminate all risk or control every influence. That is not possible. Your job is to stay present, pay attention, and keep the lines of communication open. When she knows you are involved, not to spy, but to support, she feels safer. When she sees that you are not afraid to ask hard questions or point out concerns, she learns to trust your perspective. And when you listen, even when you disagree, she learns that your love is steady and your wisdom is reliable.

Guarding her circle is not about building a fence around her life. It is about walking alongside her as she moves through it, offering protection, perspective, and presence. You are not standing outside her world. You are standing close enough to see the details and far enough to let her grow. That balance is what makes you a strong father in her teenage years.

Keep Showing Up: How Your Steady Presence Shapes Her Confidence

Adolescence can make connection feel elusive. Your daughter may seem distant, answer in one-word sentences, or seem lost in her own world. You might feel like nothing you say gets through, like your efforts fall flat. But what you do during these quiet, often frustrating years matters more than ever. Because while your daughter may not always say it, she still needs you. Your steady presence, especially when it is not demanded or dramatic, is one of the strongest forces shaping her confidence.

You are showing her what dependable love looks like. And in a world that often sends girls messages that they are only valued for their appearance, their popularity, or their performance, this kind of love is radical. It tells her she is enough. Not because of what she does, but because of who she is. And that is a very important message for her to understand and experience.

Small, consistent actions mean more than grand gestures. Sitting next to her on the couch, even when she's on her phone, offering to drive her, even when she could go with someone else, and asking how she slept, even when she barely responds; these moments form a quiet rhythm of care. They tell her you are there, and that you will continue to be there. That kind of consistency becomes part of how she sees herself. It builds an internal sense of worth.

When your daughter knows you will show up, day after day, without needing her to perform or entertain you, it teaches her that relationships can be safe and secure. That men can be trustworthy. That love can be stable and respectful. Even if she does not say thank you now, even if she shrugs you off, she is storing those moments. They become the emotional ground she stands on when life gets difficult.

This does not mean you have to be perfect. You will lose your temper. You will misread signals. You will say the wrong thing. What matters is that you keep coming back. Apologize when needed. Try again when a conversation falls flat. Laugh with her when you can. Ask her to teach you something about her world, her music, or her favorite show; something that makes her feel seen. These small invitations help her know that her inner life matters to you, even when she is not ready to share all of it.

Sometimes presence means knowing when to step back. Teenagers often need space to process emotions, make mistakes, and learn on their own. Respecting that space while remaining emotionally available takes strength. You do not need to push your way in. But you can keep the door open. You can say, "I'm around if you feel like talking," or "I just wanted you to know I love you." These small words remind her that you are not going anywhere.

There may be long stretches where it feels like you are being ignored. Keep showing up. Keep checking in. Even when it feels one-sided. Because in those moments, you are sending a message she will remember years from now: that love shows up, that you show up, even when it is not easy.

The truth is, your presence in her life is not a background detail. It is part of her identity. She is learning how to feel safe, how to feel worthy, and how to believe in herself. And those lessons often come not from big talks, but from your daily commitment to being there.

So keep showing up. Not because it always feels good or easy. But because that's what strong fathers do. And because your presence today is building the woman she will become tomorrow.

Chapter Five

Lead By Example

The best way to teach your daughter to expect respect from others is to show it to her yourself. You are her first true love; the first man to show her what care, consistency, and dignity look like. When you invest in her, speak to her with respect, and value her deeply, she learns not to settle for anything less in her future relationships.

She's Watching You: The First Man She Ever Learns From

From the very beginning, your daughter looks to you to understand what it means to be loved by a man. Long before she ever goes on a date, long before the topic of relationships even comes up, she is already learning from you, watching how you treat the people around you, how you handle conflict, how you express emotion, and how you talk about women. She's absorbing it all. Whether you realize it or not, you are the first blueprint for love, respect, and masculinity that she will ever encounter. And what she learns from you will shape her beliefs about what is normal, what is acceptable, and what she deserves.

This influence is not about delivering lectures or giving warnings about boys. It is not about telling her what kind of man to look for one day. It is about showing her, through your own behavior, what kind of treatment is right and what kind of behavior should never be tolerated. If you treat her with kindness and respect, if you listen to her thoughts without dismissing them, and if you take an interest in her world, even when it doesn't match your own, then you are setting a powerful example. She learns that her voice matters. She learns that men can be emotionally present, protective, and safe.

But if you dismiss her emotions, interrupt her when she speaks, tease her in ways that hurt, or walk out when things get difficult, she learns something else. She learns to expect distance. She learns to keep things inside. She learns that maybe love has to come with a cost. And the tragic truth is, many girls who grow up without a healthy father figure, either through absence or emotional neglect, later struggle to identify red flags in relationships. They accept poor treatment because no one showed them what love was supposed to look like.

Your role is not to be perfect. It is to be intentional. Every moment is an opportunity to teach her what healthy manhood looks like. She is watching how you respond when you are frustrated. She notices whether you take responsibility when you are wrong. She pays attention to whether you speak kindly of others, whether you're generous with your time, and whether you follow through on your word. These daily examples are far more powerful than any rule you set or advice you give.

If you lose your temper, apologize. Let her see that strength includes accountability. If you're tired but she wants to talk, put down your phone and listen. Let her feel that her thoughts matter, not just when they're convenient, but always. If she's excited to show you something—even if it's a silly meme or a new dance, celebrate that moment. Your interest tells her that what she values is worth your attention.

This is especially important when she begins to express opinions that differ from yours. As she grows, she will develop her own voice, and she will sometimes challenge what you believe. When that happens, stay calm. Listen. Ask questions. Don't belittle her thinking or talk over her. By engaging with her respectfully, you are teaching her that she deserves respect in return, even when there is disagreement. You are modeling emotional safety. That is something no future partner should ever be allowed to violate.

She is also learning from how you interact with others outside the home. If you flirt with strangers, make sexist jokes, or treat women as objects, she is learning something from that. She may not say anything, but it will register. It will become part of the puzzle she is assembling about relationships and self-worth. On the other hand, if you speak to women with dignity, if you uplift and defend them, they will come to expect the same level of respect in their own relationships.

She is even learning from how you handle silence. When you come home from work and you're quiet or distant, when you're physically present but emotionally withdrawn, she notices. You don't have to always be talkative or cheerful, but you do need to be emotionally available. You can say, "I had a hard day," or "I'm feeling tired, but I still want to hear about your day." You are teaching her that real men do not shut down when life gets hard; they stay connected.

Sometimes, fathers think they can wait until their daughters are older to start modeling these things. But by then, the habits are already formed. Your influence starts the day she is born. And it doesn't end when she hits adolescence. Your consistency during her teenage years is what helps her form the emotional backbone she will carry into adulthood. If she learns that love is gentle, strong, respectful, and honest, she will not settle for less. If she sees that being a man includes empathy, accountability, and presence, she will look for that in others.

Your daughter may not always act like she's watching. She may seem indifferent, distracted, or distant. But make no mistake, she is taking mental notes. She is building a quiet list of what is normal, what is possible, and what she can hope for in her future. The more you live with intention and integrity, the stronger that foundation becomes.

So show her. Show her what it looks like to love someone well. Show her what calm leadership sounds like. Show her how a real man handles fear, frustration, disappointment, and joy. Show her what it means to protect, not control. And above all, show her that the kind of man she deserves is not a fantasy. He is real. He exists. Because he raised her.

Love Her Mother Well: The Relationship She Will Measure Against

Whether you are married to your daughter's mother, divorced, remarried, or co-parenting from afar, one thing remains true: your daughter is watching how you treat her mother. That relationship, whatever its form, will become her reference point for what is normal in love. The tone you set, the words you choose, the way you show up, or don't, all of it becomes the foundation for how she will allow others to treat her in the future.

Many fathers do not realize how much power they hold in shaping their daughter's future relationships through this one area. They think, "She doesn't really notice," or, "It's between her mother and me." But children are observant. Daughters, in particular, pay attention to the emotional climate between their parents. She watches your tone when you disagree with her. She notices if you roll your eyes, shut down, or lash out. She sees if you listen when her mother speaks, or if you brush her off. These moments are not invisible. They are formative.

If your relationship with your daughter's mother is strong and healthy, you are already modeling something profoundly valuable. She sees love as including respect, affection, shared responsibility, and open communication. She sees that disagreements can be handled with grace and repair. She witnesses partnership, not power struggles. Even small gestures, such as saying thank you, showing physical affection, and being present for family meals, can teach her that love is active and intentional.

If the relationship is strained, your opportunity to teach is no less important. In fact, it may matter even more. You may not be able to control how her mother behaves or communicates, but you *can* control how you respond to her. You can choose to be respectful, even when things are tense. You can choose to speak well of her mother in front of your daughter. You can take the high road, especially when it is hard. That decision, made again and again, tells your daughter: love can remain respectful, even when relationships change.

Divorced fathers sometimes believe their influence has diminished because they are no longer under the same roof. But this is not true. In fact, how you treat your ex-wife or co-parent becomes a powerful lesson in emotional maturity. If your daughter sees that you cooperate, communicate calmly, and show up consistently for her, even when it requires coordination and compromise, she learns what emotional responsibility looks like. She learns that respect does not end when a marriage does. That is a lesson many adults never receive, and you can be the one to give it to her.

The way you talk about your daughter's mother, especially in moments of frustration, will stay with your daughter long after the words are spoken. Speaking harshly about her mother, even if it feels justified, puts your daughter in an impossible position. She is connected to both of you. Criticizing her mother forces her to split her loyalty. It introduces shame, guilt, and emotional confusion. Even when she seems angry at her mother, even when she vents, your role is not to pile on. Your role is to be steady. To listen. To redirect the conversation with grace. You can say, "I know that was hard," or "It's okay to feel upset," without adding more negativity. This keeps your daughter emotionally safe.

More than anything, your daughter is watching for consistency. If you say you respect her mother but speak over her in public, that contradiction teaches her something about double standards. If you demand respect from your daughter but model condescension toward your partner, she learns that respect is conditional. If you only act civil when someone is watching, she learns that love is performance. But if you stay grounded, patient, kind, and engaged, through both smooth and stormy moments, she learns that love is rooted in character.

This modeling extends into the daily routines of life. If you are married or in a relationship, your daughter will notice whether you contribute at home, whether you parent together, and whether you show appreciation for each other. She sees the balance of emotional labor. She feels the emotional tone. When you ask your partner how her day was, when you step in without being asked, when you protect time to be together as a family, these are not small things; they are messages about what love looks like when it is real and enduring.

If you are parenting solo or your relationship with her mother is truly strained, you can still model dignity. Keep your commitments. Avoid speaking negatively. Let your daughter hear you say things like, "Your mom and I both love you," or, "We may not always agree, but we both want what's best for you." These statements show maturity.

They teach her that conflict does not require cruelty, and that love can still be honored even when it is no longer romantic.

There is also an opportunity to talk about relationships more broadly. Share what you've learned over the years, what you got right, what you wish you had done differently. Be honest about your growth. Say things like, "I used to think love meant solving every problem, but now I know it means listening more." Or, "I've learned that respect matters more than always being right." These conversations will stay with her. They will shape what she expects and what she is willing to accept.

Ultimately, your daughter is not just learning how to be loved. She is learning what it means to love someone else. She is learning about mutual respect, shared responsibility, and emotional safety. If she grows up watching her father treat her mother with dignity, she will not settle for a relationship built on control, fear, or neglect. She will recognize the difference, not because someone told her, but because someone showed her.

So love her mother well. Whether it is from within the same home or across two different households, do it with consistency, respect, and emotional steadiness. Because the way you love her mother is not just shaping your daughter's expectations; it is shaping her future.

Show Her What Strength Really Looks Like

Strength is one of the most misunderstood traits we pass down to our children. For generations, strength in fathers was defined by toughness, silence, or a refusal to show vulnerability. Many men were taught that to lead a family meant hiding emotions, pushing through pain, and never showing weakness. But daughters do not need that kind of strength. What they need is the kind of strength that builds trust, models humility, and protects without controlling. They need to see what real emotional strength looks like, and they are looking to you to show them.

Your daughter is growing up in a world full of mixed messages. She sees images of power that often involve dominance, control, or emotional detachment. She sees relationships where strength is confused with being louder, colder, or more intimidating. But you can give her a different image. You can show her that true strength is not about who talks the most, who controls the room, or who wins every argument. True strength is measured in character, in how you respond when things are difficult, how you treat people when no one is watching, and how you stay grounded when emotions run high.

Start with self-control. If you lose your temper often, if you yell or withdraw, or if you become sarcastic or cold when you are frustrated, your daughter may learn that anger is what power looks like. She may grow to accept emotional volatility as normal. But when you remain calm under pressure, when you take a breath before reacting, when you show her that emotions can be felt without being acted out destructively, you are showing her something better. You are modeling emotional maturity.

This does not mean suppressing your feelings. In fact, sharing your emotions, honestly, appropriately, and calmly, is one of the most powerful things you can do as a father. If you had a hard day, say so. If you are feeling stressed, let her know. If something moved you to tears, do not hide it. When your daughter sees you own your emotions without shame, she learns that strength includes vulnerability. She learns that men can feel deeply and still lead well. She learns that her father is strong, and she, too, is becoming strong.

Accountability is another cornerstone of real strength. If you mess up, apologize. If you say something you regret, name it. If you are distracted and miss something important, acknowledge it. These moments are not signs of weakness. They are signs of integrity. A man who can take responsibility for his mistakes is a man others can trust. And a daughter who sees this will carry the same expectation into her own relationships. She will learn that real love does not hide behind ego. It takes ownership. It repairs when needed.

Strength also means being steady. Not perfect, not always cheerful, but steady. Your presence should be something she can count on. She should know that when life is hard, you will not disappear emotionally. That you will be calm in the chaos. That you will still listen, still show up, still be there even when she is difficult, distant, or angry. This steadiness becomes part of her sense of safety. It tells her that she is not too much to handle, that she does not have to hide when things fall apart.

How you speak to others, especially in moments of tension, also teaches your daughter what strength sounds like. Do you belittle people when they make mistakes? Do you speak with contempt? Do you interrupt or talk over others? Or do you practice patience? Do you speak clearly and firmly without raising your voice? Do you listen as much as you speak? These patterns shape her understanding of how healthy men communicate. They shape her expectations for what respect should feel like.

When you model this kind of strength, your daughter not only feels safe, but she also grows stronger herself. She learns that she can have opinions, express emotions, and set boundaries. She learns that her voice matters. And she learns that she is worthy of being treated with care and respect.

There is also strength in how you handle failure. Whether it is a mistake at work, a disagreement in your marriage, or a decision you wish you had made differently, your response to failure teaches her what resilience really is. If you shut down, blame others, or spiral into shame, she may come to fear failure. But if you reflect, adjust, and move forward with humility, she will see that strength is not about being flawless. It is about being willing to grow.

Service is another form of strength that often goes unspoken. When you help without being asked, when you show up early, when you sacrifice time or convenience for your family, you are teaching her that strength is not selfish. It is generous. And in a world where many girls are told they should shrink themselves to please others, your example shows her that love does not ask her to disappear. It asks her to rise, to be seen, to be respected.

All of this begins with you. The way you carry yourself, the way you hold your ground, and the way you treat people all become her internal guide. She will carry your example into friendships, into partnerships, and eventually, into marriage. She may not quote your words, but she will remember your presence. She will remember the steadiness in your voice when she felt unsure. She will remember the way you honored others, and the way you honored yourself.

Strong fathers show their daughters what strength truly means, not through control or silence, but through integrity, presence, and emotional courage. Your example gives her a reference point she can return to again and again, especially when life presents her with choices that test her worth. If she has seen what real strength looks like, she will not be fooled by cheap imitations. And when the time comes for her to choose a partner, she will not be guessing. She will not be settling. She will be measuring every relationship against the quiet, unwavering strength you demonstrated every day.

Set the Standard So She Never Settles

Every father wonders at some point what kind of man his daughter will one day fall in love with. Will he treat her with kindness? Will he respect her boundaries? Will he value her thoughts, her strength, and her dreams? These are questions rooted in love and concern, but they are not questions you leave to chance. The truth is, one of the most powerful influences on who your daughter will choose and what she will tolerate is the standard you set while she is still growing up.

You are shaping her expectations, not just for love, but for how she should be treated in every relationship. If she grows up seeing a father who is consistent, respectful, emotionally present, and kind, she will instinctively look for those qualities in others. If she grows up with a father who listens when she speaks, shows up when it matters, and honors his commitments, she will learn to expect nothing less. And if she grows up watching a man who models integrity, who leads with calm strength instead of control, she will develop a quiet but unshakable belief: "I am worthy of respect."

However, if she witnesses the opposite, if she sees you dismiss people, raise your voice when things don't go your way, break promises, or exhibit emotional distance, she may come to believe that this is how relationships typically work. She may not like it, but she will feel familiar with it. And familiarity is powerful. That is how too many girls end up in relationships that echo the pain they saw growing up. It doesn't have to be abuse to be damaging. Indifference, impatience, and emotional coldness also leave their marks.

That's why your role is not just to love her. It is to lead her. To hold a higher standard in your own life so that she can build one for herself. And that starts with how you treat her. Every time you stop what you are doing to listen, you're telling her, "Your voice matters." Every time you speak to her with gentleness, even when you are correcting her, you're teaching her, "Love does not require fear." Every time you follow through on your word, you're showing her, "You can count on me, and you deserve that from others, too."

As she gets older, your daughter will be exposed to a world that often tries to lower that standard. Social media, pop culture, and even some of her peers may tell her to settle for attention over respect, chemistry over character, or appearance over connection. She may feel pressure to prove her worth or earn love through pleasing others. That is why your voice and example matter so deeply. She needs to see what it looks like when love is solid, respectful, and real. She needs to know that she never has to beg for affection, prove her value, or shrink herself to be accepted.

Talk to her about what she deserves, not as a list of rules, but as a reflection of how she should feel in a relationship. Loved. Safe. Respected. Heard. Encourage her to ask questions, trust her instincts, and speak up when something doesn't feel right. If she starts dating, do not react with fear or control. Stay curious. Ask how she feels around him. Does she feel more like herself, or less? Can she speak freely, or does she feel pressure to perform? These conversations teach her to think deeply about her choices and to value herself enough to walk away from what is unhealthy.

But these words mean little if your actions do not support them. You can tell her she deserves respect, but if you treat her mother harshly, the message is lost. You can say she should be confident, but if you only notice her when she gets good grades or looks pretty, she will associate her worth with performance. You can say she should stand up for herself, but if you shut her down when she disagrees with you, she will learn to stay silent. The standard must begin with your behavior.

This also means you have to do your own work. You must challenge any parts of yourself that are impatient, passive, or emotionally unavailable. You have to ask: What am I modeling right now?

Am I showing her how to handle conflict well? Am I demonstrating self-respect? Am I giving her an image of masculinity that is worth emulating, or one she will spend years recovering from? These are hard questions, but they are the right ones. Because setting the standard is not a one-time act, it is a lifelong commitment.

Let her see you grow. Let her hear you say, "I've learned from my mistakes." Let her witness you learning how to love better, listen better, and live with more presence. This shows her that maturity is not about having it all figured out; it's about being willing to grow. And that will give her permission to grow as well.

One day, she will walk into a relationship with someone who wants to be close to her. When that day comes, you want her to measure that person's character against everything you showed her was possible. You want her to say, "My dad never raised his voice at me," or, "My father respected me enough to listen," or, "I know what love looks like, and this doesn't feel right." That kind of internal compass doesn't come from lectures. It comes from years of quiet modeling, of leading with love and consistency.

Your job is not to protect her from every bad relationship. Your job is to show her what a good one looks like so clearly that she can see the difference. To raise the bar so high with your own behavior that anything less becomes unthinkable. You are not just building her confidence. You are building her standard.

And when you set the standard, she will carry it. She will remember what it felt like to be treated with respect, not because she read it in a book or heard it in a movie, but because she lived it with you.

Chapter Six

Risk Leads to Strength

Trying is how children grow, but for many girls, the fear of making mistakes starts early and runs deep. As her father, you have the unique power to teach your daughter that bravery is not about being perfect; it is about being willing to try. It is about being willing to risk. This chapter is about helping her take that first step, again and again, with confidence, curiosity, and the unshakable knowledge that she is supported no matter the outcome.

Build a Safe Space to Try

Courage begins in the places where a child feels most secure. For your daughter, that place is often at home, in the everyday interactions she has with you. When a father consistently shows up with empathy, patience, and encouragement, he creates an emotional foundation strong enough to support risk-taking, bold ideas, and brave beginnings. Before she ever steps into a classroom, onto a sports field, or onto a stage, she needs to feel that home is the one place she can fall and be caught with compassion.

Trying anything new involves vulnerability. Whether your daughter is learning to ride a bike, starting a new school year, or experimenting with writing a story, there will be moments of uncertainty and self-doubt. She might ask herself, "What if I mess up? What if I look silly? What if I fail?" When those questions arise, your response can shape how she answers them. If you respond with openness and calm, she will learn to approach the unknown with curiosity rather than fear. She will come to understand that mistakes are not signs of weakness but essential parts of the learning process.

Creating a safe space to try begins with how you react to her struggles. If she spills a glass of milk while learning to pour, take a breath and smile. Say, "It's okay, we all spill sometimes. Let's clean it up together." If she brings home a lower grade than expected, resist the urge to express disappointment or offer immediate solutions. Instead, ask questions that center on her experience: "What did you enjoy about this assignment? What do you think you could do differently next time?" These types of conversations shift the focus from shame or pressure to reflection and growth.

Your physical presence matters too. When you sit beside her as she attempts something new, whether it's a puzzle, a science experiment, or practicing a speech, you are silently communicating that she is not alone. You are showing her that support does not mean solving things for her. You are showing her that support is about being there as she figures it out herself. Even small rituals, like checking in after school or reading side by side before bed, reinforce the idea that your relationship is steady and that your attention is a constant she can count on.

It is also important to teach her that effort is something worth celebrating. Create small family rituals that reward trying, not just succeeding. For example, once a week, go around the dinner table and ask everyone to share one thing they tried that week, even if it did not work out. When she hears that her father struggled with something at work or tried a new skill and made mistakes, she learns that trying is not just for children. It is for everyone. These stories become a shared language in your family; a way to say, "We value effort, not perfection."

Allow her to feel frustrated or disappointed without rushing to cheer her up. There is strength in sitting with discomfort and knowing that it does not have to be fixed right away. Let her vent after a hard day. Reflect back what you hear: "It sounds like you felt left out," or "That must have been frustrating." Let the moment breathe. Then, when the time is right, ask her what she wants to do next. Giving her the space to process her feelings and decide her next steps helps her build emotional resilience.

You can also create a physical environment that encourages trying. Keep simple materials on hand, such as blocks, craft supplies, science kits, and musical instruments. Let her explore without a specific outcome in mind. If she builds a tower and it collapses, say, "That was a strong design. What might make it even stronger next time?" These types of environments teach her that experimenting is fun and worthwhile, even if the result is messy or incomplete.

Teach her that asking for help is not a sign of weakness, but rather a sign of strength. When you model this in your own life, reaching out to a neighbor, reading instructions aloud, or asking her for help with something, you show her that no one has to figure everything out alone. Encourage her to reach out to teachers, coaches, or friends when she needs support. Teach her to self-advocate. Help her understand that courage and connection often go hand in hand.

Above all, remind her daily through your words and actions that her worth is not tied to her performance. She does not need to earn your pride or your love. It is already hers. She is not valued for being perfect but for being present, persistent, and engaged. When she knows this at her core, she will begin to take the kinds of risks that lead to real growth.

Model Risk-Taking and Normalize Mistakes

Children learn far more from what we do than from what we say. If you want your daughter to become someone who takes risks, tries new things, and views failure as a stepping stone to growth, then she needs to see those values reflected in you. As a father, you are her first and most consistent role model. She watches how you respond to frustration, how you handle uncertainty, and how you deal with things not going as planned. Every time you respond with calm, curiosity, and a willingness to try again, you teach her that she can do the same.

Modeling risk-taking does not require you to take up skydiving or start a business; it simply involves understanding the risks associated with various activities. It begins in your everyday life. Let her see you tackle something unfamiliar: fixing something around the house, cooking a new recipe, trying a new technology, or starting a hobby you have no prior experience in. Instead of hiding your mistakes, talk about them openly. When something does not go as expected, narrate your process: "I thought that would work, but I see now I made an error. I'm going to try a different way." This shows her that mistakes are not dead ends, but rather part of the process.

When children grow up believing that adults are supposed to have all the answers, they feel pressure to avoid mistakes at all costs. But when they see adults learning in real-time, fumbling, adjusting, and reflecting, they realize that learning is a lifelong process. That mindset frees them to take more chances. When your daughter sees that you do not have to be perfect to be capable, she begins to let go of the need for perfection herself.

Let your daughter be part of your trial-and-error process. Ask her for input when you are unsure about something. Let her help with the instructions for assembling a new piece of furniture or choosing ingredients for a new dish. Ask her what she thinks might work. When her suggestion helps, celebrate it. When it doesn't, thank her anyway and discuss what you both learned; these moments show her that she can contribute and that trying, even when it does not lead to immediate success, is always valuable.

Laugh at your mistakes. When your "great idea" turns into a disaster or you misplace something, be willing to laugh at yourself and move on. Humor is one of the most effective tools for defusing shame. It teaches your daughter that making a mistake is not a personal failure; it is just part of being human. When she sees you remain light-hearted in the face of setbacks, she learns that mistakes do not have to be scary.

Celebrate your own efforts out loud. Say things like, "I am proud of myself for finishing that even though it was hard," or, "I stuck with that longer than I thought I could." These reflections reinforce a growth mindset in your home. They show that persistence and problem-solving are worthy of recognition, regardless of the final result.

When something you try doesn't go well, talk about how you recovered. Maybe a work project failed or a goal fell through. Share how you handled it emotionally and practically. This gives your daughter language and context for when she encounters her own disappointments. Say things like, "I was really disappointed at first, but I took a break, made a new plan, and reached out for help."

Be willing to try things with her that are new for both of you. Sign up for a class together, build something from scratch, or take on a shared project. When she sees you learning alongside her, it flattens the hierarchy. It sends the message that you are partners in growth.

Finally, be patient with your own learning curve. Let her see that it takes time to improve, that success often comes after many tries, and that perseverance is more important than talent. Your openness and honesty will teach her to be kinder to herself and more willing to take risks and step into the unknown.

Celebrate Effort, Curiosity, and Strategy

In a culture that too often prizes outcomes, awards, and perfection, children can start to believe that only results matter. This belief can erode their confidence and make them hesitant to start unless they are certain they can win. For girls, especially, research shows that fear of failure often sets in earlier than it does for boys. They may start holding back, sticking to what they already know they can do well, and avoiding anything that feels uncertain. As a father, you can help shift this mindset by showing her that it is not the outcome that defines success, but rather the effort, strategy, and courage it takes to try.

The way you talk about her challenges matters deeply. Instead of saying, "You are so smart," focus on her persistence and process. Say, "You worked really hard on that," or, "I love how you stuck with that even when it got frustrating." These kinds of affirmations build a growth mindset. They teach her that her abilities are not fixed but can grow with effort, creativity, and time. She learns that mistakes are not proof of weakness; they are evidence of learning and growth.

Praise her curiosity. When she asks a hundred questions or takes things apart to see how they work, support her instinct to explore. Ask her questions in return. Say, "That is a great question. What do you think?" or, "Let's look that up together." Help her see that curiosity is a strength, not a nuisance. The more you encourage her to wonder, to notice, and to investigate, the more confident she will become in her own thinking.

Strategy is just as important as effort. When she solves a problem or approaches something from a new angle, be sure to point that out. Say, "I noticed how you tried a different way to build that tower," or, "It was smart how you asked for help when you got stuck." These comments help her understand that how she tackles a challenge matters. She begins to internalize that the process is where the real growth happens.

It is also important to create space for trial and error. Give her the freedom to explore projects that may not yield results, whether it's writing a story, building a contraption, or designing something from scraps. Do not pressure her to finish or to make it perfect. Let her walk away if she wants, and come back later with a new idea. This shows her that creativity is a cycle, not a checklist.

In your home, highlight stories of people who tried and failed and kept going. Read biographies of inventors, athletes, artists, and scientists who faced setbacks. Watch documentaries together that show the behind-the-scenes effort behind success. Discuss what they had to overcome. Help her see that every success story is built on persistence, trial, and resilience.

Try starting a "challenge journal" where she can jot down things she has attempted, what worked, what didn't, and what she learned. You can do the same. Compare notes and talk about what surprises came from the process. This makes effort visible and gives you both a shared language around growth and self-discovery.

Be intentional about the words you use when she struggles. Instead of jumping in to solve the problem, ask open-ended questions: "What have you tried so far?" or "What do you think would happen if you tried it a different way?" Offer support, but let her lead. The confidence she builds by finding her own way forward will stay with her much longer than a quick fix.

At school, she may feel pressure to get high grades or meet expectations. At home, let her feel the opposite, let her know she can breathe, explore, and even fall apart a little without fear. That sense of safety is what allows her to experiment and grow.

Celebrate small milestones. Cheer her on when she speaks up for herself, learns a new skill, or completes a project she once thought was too hard. Remind her how far she has come. This helps her see progress over time and recognize her own capacity to adapt and improve.

By consistently praising effort, curiosity, and strategy, you give your daughter the tools she needs to face life's challenges with confidence. You teach her that success is not about being right the first time, but about being brave enough to begin and persistent enough to keep going.

Expand Her Vision of What's Possible

A girl cannot dream beyond what she has seen. That does not mean she needs to witness the exact version of her future, but she does need to see examples of courage, strength, and leadership reflected in the lives of women. As her father, you play a key role in making sure she knows that women can do anything, not just because you tell her so, but because you show her. The stories you share, the media you consume together, and the people you admire all shape her sense of what is possible.

Start by making women's achievements visible in your daily life. Watch women's sports with enthusiasm. Cheer for the athletes and talk about the hard work, strategy, and dedication that got them there. Make it as normal to watch a WNBA game or the Women's World Cup as it is to watch men's sports. Let your daughter see that you value female athletes just as much as male ones.

Seek out books and films that highlight girls and women who are bold, smart, and determined. Whether it is a fictional character like Moana or Matilda, or a real-life hero like Jane Goodall, Mae Jemison, or Malala Yousafzai, share their stories. Talk about what they faced, how they responded, and what your daughter notices about their courage. These stories stick. They become part of the backdrop she draws from when she begins to imagine her own path.

Bring her into spaces where women are in leadership roles. That might mean attending a community event, hearing a female speaker, or touring a workplace where women are represented in fields such as engineering, medicine, architecture, or entrepreneurship. Exposure builds confidence. When she sees women solving problems, leading meetings, or speaking with authority, she begins to imagine herself in those roles too.

Encourage her to ask questions and speak up. When you are out in the world together, invite her to order her own food, talk to shopkeepers, or ask questions at the museum. Stand beside her, but let her take the lead. The more practice she gets being assertive and curious, the more naturally it will come.

Talk about the invisible work women do. If your daughter sees her mother, teacher, or another woman managing multiple tasks, name that effort. Say, "Did you notice how your mom planned the whole trip and made sure everyone had what they needed? That takes serious skill." Help her see the intelligence, organization, and care behind everyday actions.

Be honest about inequality, too, in age-appropriate ways. When something unfair happens to a woman in a movie or real life, ask her what she thinks. Talk about why it matters. Let her know that while the world is changing, there is still work to be done, and that she can be part of that change. Teach her that advocacy and fairness are part of strength.

Encourage her to lead, even in small ways. Let her plan a family outing, run a lemonade stand, or start a book club with friends. These experiences teach her that leadership is not about power; it is about vision, effort, and courage.

Most importantly, be consistent in how you value and speak about women. Your attitude toward the women in your life: how you talk to them, how you speak about them, and how you support them, will influence your daughter more than anything you say directly to her. Treat women with respect, admiration, and fairness. Let her see you listening, learning, and supporting others.

When you expand your daughter's view of what is possible, you do more than inspire her. You prepare her. You prepare her with examples, tools, and confidence that she will carry into adulthood. She will not just dream about trying new things; she will believe she can.

By building a safe space, modeling bravery, celebrating effort, and widening her world, you teach your daughter the most powerful lesson of all: she is allowed to try, she is allowed to fail, and she is strong enough to begin again.

Chapter Seven

Raising a Daughter Who Speaks Up

Strong women have voices, and they are not afraid to use them. They know how to stand up for themselves, speak their truth, and protect their well-being with confidence and clarity. As a strong father, it is your responsibility to teach your daughter these skills, starting with how she uses her voice at home. When you encourage her to express herself without fear, you lay the foundation for self-respect that will follow her for life. The way you listen, show her respect, respond, and create space for her voice now will shape how boldly she speaks in every room she enters.

Your Voice Becomes Her Inner Voice

The way you speak to her shapes how she speaks to herself and others. Your words, whether you realize it or not, echo in your daughter's heart long after they leave your mouth. The way you speak to her today becomes the way she speaks to herself tomorrow. If your voice is calm, steady, and respectful, even when correcting her, she will grow up believing she deserves to be spoken to that way. If your words affirm her worth and validate her perspective, she will come to believe that her thoughts and feelings matter. And that belief will shape how she carries herself in the world.

Fathers often underestimate just how powerful their words are in shaping a daughter's identity. She listens not only to what you say, but how you say it. Your tone, your body language, your eye contact; these subtle cues send constant messages about whether she is valued, heard, and understood. If she grows up in a home where her voice is received with interest and respect, she'll learn to trust that her words have meaning. She'll internalize the idea that it's not only safe to speak up, but right to speak up.

On the other hand, when a father dismisses, interrupts, talks over, or minimizes his daughter's expressions, he is diminishing her and teaching her to stay quiet. Even subtle forms of invalidation, like laughing at her ideas, brushing off her emotions, or constantly "correcting" her thoughts, can chip away at her confidence to speak her truth. Over time, she may begin to silence herself before anyone else can. She may begin to doubt whether her voice matters at all.

You want her to walk into every room with her head high, to speak with conviction, and to stand her ground when necessary. That begins with you; at your dinner table, in your car rides, and during your bedtime conversations. When she tells you a story and you lean in and listen, she learns her voice holds attention. When she disagrees with you and you thank her for sharing her honest thoughts, she learns that respect and disagreement can coexist. When she's overwhelmed and your voice stays calm instead of reactive, she learns how to stay grounded even while feeling strong emotions.

You don't have to be perfect. What matters most is that your voice reflects love, safety, and respect. That she hears more encouragement than criticism, more curiosity than control, more understanding than correction. The more often your words tell her "you are smart," "you are capable," "your feelings matter," the more likely she is to repeat those same truths to herself when you're not around.

Eventually, she'll face moments when her voice is tested, at school, in friendships, in future relationships, or in the workplace. In those moments, it's not just her courage that will show up. It's the voice she's carried with her since childhood. It's the internal message she learned from you about what she deserves and what she's allowed to say out loud.

The goal here is to raise her in a way that she knows that her voice matters in every room she walks into. To teach her that those who do not show her and treat her with respect (especially men) are not worthy of her. The best way to do this is to be the best male role model you can be and show her respect, encourage her to speak her mind respectfully and powerfully, and teach her to stand up for herself.

So, let your voice be the steady one she hears when she doubts herself. Let it be the firm but loving voice that taught her she can speak without shrinking. Let it be the voice that shaped a self-assured young woman who knows her worth and isn't afraid to say so.

Because in the end, your words will become part of her inner world. And if you choose them wisely, your voice will become the foundation she stands on, the strength she draws from, and the echo that reminds her she never has to be silent.

Create Safe Spaces for Her to Express Herself

Listening without judgment builds the confidence to speak boldly in the world. If you want your daughter to grow into a young woman who uses her voice with strength and certainty, she first needs to feel safe using it with you. That safety is not built by accident. It is built through intentional choices, how you listen, how you respond, and how consistently you show her that her thoughts and emotions are welcomed, not judged.

Creating a safe space does not mean agreeing with everything she says. It means letting her know that her words will be met with respect, even when they challenge you or make you uncomfortable. When a daughter knows her father will not dismiss, mock, or explode in reaction to her honesty, she begins to relax into her voice. She no longer speaks to defend or please; she speaks to connect, to reflect, and to be known.

Fathers often want to protect, correct, and fix their children, especially their daughters. These instincts come from a place of love. But when a daughter opens up about something vulnerable, what she often needs first is not advice or a solution, but presence. She needs you to sit with her in her experience without trying to shape it. She needs you to listen, not to respond, but to understand.

When your daughter tells you about something she is afraid of, upset by, or unsure about, resist the urge to minimize it. What seems small to you might feel enormous to her. When she tells you about a friend who hurt her feelings or a teacher who embarrassed her, pause before jumping in with solutions. First, acknowledge what you heard. Say things like, "That sounds really hard," or "I can see why you'd feel that way." These simple responses create an emotional anchor. They teach her that her feelings make sense, that her experiences are valid, and that her voice has weight.

It is also important to create time and space for her to speak. Not every conversation needs to happen in a moment of crisis or urgency. Some of the most honest things your daughter will share might occur during a quiet car ride, a walk around the neighborhood, or while sitting on the edge of her bed at night. These in-between moments are golden opportunities. They feel low-pressure, low-stakes, and emotionally accessible. Be present in them. Ask open-ended questions. Show her that you are not just willing to hear her, but that you are truly interested.

When she feels safe to express herself at home, she will begin to trust her ability to express herself in the world. She will raise her hand in class, speak up when something feels wrong, and ask for what she needs without guilt. That confidence does not come from being told to be brave; it comes from having the space to practice, over and over again, in the safety of her relationship with you.

Safe spaces also require consistency. If you are warm and receptive one day, then critical or impatient the next, she will learn to guard herself. She will begin to choose her words carefully, not out of wisdom, but out of fear. The goal is not perfection; it is predictability. Your daughter should know that no matter what she brings to you: joy, frustration, confusion, or hurt, your response will be rooted in care.

You are her emotional training ground. The way you respond to her words teaches her what to expect from others. If you listen attentively, she will learn to expect to be heard. If you treat her voice with respect, she will grow to demand respect from those around her. And if you make room for her whole self, messy, curious, and evolving, she will learn to take up space without apology.

The gift of a safe space is not just about communication; it is about identity. It tells your daughter that her truth matters. That she does not have to perform or be perfect to be accepted. That her voice is not a threat, but a tool for connection, self-expression, and strength.

And when a girl learns that at home, she carries it with her for the rest of her life.

Encourage Her to Ask, Challenge, and Disagree

Raising a daughter who knows her opinion matters, even when it's unpopular, is the foundation of building strength. One of the most powerful things a father can teach his daughter is that her voice matters, even when it does not align with what others want to hear. Encouraging your daughter to speak up, ask questions, and respectfully challenge ideas builds the foundation for lifelong confidence. It teaches her that she is allowed to think critically, hold firm to her values, and communicate her needs with clarity and strength.

This kind of courage does not happen automatically. It must be nurtured, step by step, in a home where disagreement is not punished but welcomed and encouraged. Many girls are socialized to avoid conflict, smooth things over, and maintain peace, often at the expense of their own opinions. If they are constantly corrected or shut down when they challenge authority or offer a different perspective, they will begin to silence themselves. Over time, this can turn into people-pleasing, passive behavior, or a deep discomfort with self-expression.

As her father, you are in a unique position to change that pattern. When you invite your daughter into conversations where she can express herself openly, you show her that her ideas have value. You teach her that her voice is not just acceptable but essential. When she disagrees with you and you respond with curiosity rather than frustration, you model emotional maturity and respect. You show her that relationships can hold differences without collapsing under them.

Encouraging her to ask questions is just as important. Whether she is five or fifteen, make room for her curiosity. If she asks why a rule exists or why something is done a certain way, avoid responding with "because I said so." Instead, take the time to explain your reasoning, and if appropriate, invite her thoughts. This signals that you value her mind, and that her perspective is worth hearing. It also teaches her how to engage with others thoughtfully, even when she disagrees with them.

Challenge can be uncomfortable, especially when it comes from someone you love and are trying to guide. But your daughter's ability to challenge you is not a sign of disrespect. It is a sign that she feels emotionally safe enough to be honest. If she can express disagreement with you, she is learning the skills she will need to advocate for herself in friendships, relationships, and professional settings. She is learning how to be assertive without being aggressive, how to communicate clearly without shutting down, and how to honor her inner voice even when it goes against the grain.

It is also important to affirm her when she takes the risk to disagree or question something. Say things like, "I appreciate you sharing your thoughts," or "You made a good point." These statements may seem small, but they go a long way in reinforcing the idea that her voice holds power. When she feels heard and respected by you, she will be less likely to shrink herself in the face of peer pressure or unhealthy authority figures later in life.

Encouraging disagreement does not mean relinquishing your role as a parent or guide; it simply means being open to different perspectives. You can still set clear expectations and boundaries, but you can do so in a way that leaves space for her input. In fact, when a daughter feels included in conversations that affect her, she is more likely to respect the outcome. She does not need to win every argument, but she needs to know her thoughts are taken seriously.

Ultimately, you are teaching her how to be in the world: how to speak her truth without fear, how to stay grounded in her beliefs, and how to engage in honest conversations with strength and humility. These are not just communication skills; they are life skills. And they begin with you.

Raise a Self-Advocate, Not a People-Pleaser

It is important to help her stand up for herself without apologizing for her strength. Every father wants his daughter to be liked, respected, and treated kindly. However, too often, girls are taught that the way to achieve these things is by staying quiet, avoiding conflict, and prioritizing others' needs over their own. While kindness and empathy are important, they should never come at the cost of her self-respect. As her father, one of the greatest gifts you can give your daughter is the ability to speak up for herself, set clear boundaries, and advocate for her own needs without guilt or apology.

People-pleasing often starts early. A young girl learns that being "nice" earns approval. She sees that when she goes along with what others want, she avoids tension. Over time, she may begin to associate her worth with how well she makes others feel comfortable. She may start to believe that saying no is selfish, that asking for help is a burden, or that disagreeing means she is being difficult. These beliefs do not remain confined to childhood; they follow her into adulthood, shaping her friendships, relationships, and even her career choices.

Your role as a father is to interrupt that pattern. You can begin by making sure your daughter knows that her needs matter. When she says she is tired, do not push her past her limit. When she says no to a hug or a request, respect it. These moments might seem small, but they send a clear message: she is allowed to have limits, and those limits deserve to be honored.

Encourage her to check in with herself. Ask her how she feels about a decision instead of telling her what she should do. Teach her that it is okay to take a moment before saying yes, and that she is not responsible for keeping everyone happy. Let her know that it is possible to be kind and firm at the same time.

Modeling self-advocacy is just as important as teaching it. Let her see you say no when something is not right for you. Let her hear you speak up when a boundary has been crossed. If she sees you honoring your own needs with clarity and respect, she will learn to do the same. Children do not just absorb what we say; they absorb what we live.

When your daughter learns to advocate for herself, she becomes stronger not just in her words but in her identity. She is less likely to be taken advantage of, more likely to leave unhealthy situations, and more equipped to make decisions that align with her values. She learns to protect her time, her energy, and her emotional well-being.

That strength does not mean she will never have doubts. There will be times when she feels pressure to fit in, remain quiet, or avoid confrontation. In those moments, your voice—the one that has encouraged her, affirmed her, and reminded her of her worth—will echo in her mind. She will remember that she is not here to please everyone. She is here to live a life that is honest, whole, and aligned with who she truly is.

Praise her not just for being polite, but for being clear. Celebrate her not just for being agreeable, but for being honest. Let her know that her voice is not a problem to manage, but a power to embrace. The world will try to shrink her in a thousand subtle ways. Your job is to help her hold her ground.

Because a girl who knows how to advocate for herself becomes a woman who knows her worth, and that kind of strength, once rooted, can carry her through anything.

Chapter Eight

Physical Strength and Protection

As her father, it is your responsibility to help your daughter develop physical strength. This isn't about pushing her to become an athlete or drilling her like a soldier, but it *is* about ensuring she moves her body, builds confidence through physical challenges, and learns how to protect herself. A strong girl doesn't just feel capable, she carries herself differently, sets firmer boundaries, and is less likely to be intimidated, manipulated, or harmed. You don't need to be an expert in fitness or martial arts to get her started, but you *do* need to make strength a priority. When she learns that her body is powerful, not just decorative, everything changes.

Strength Is Her Birthright: Encouraging a Confident Relationship with Her Body

Your daughter's relationship with her body begins long before she enters adolescence. It starts with how you speak to her, how you show up for her, and what you model in terms of strength, ability, and self-respect. Too often, girls are praised for being cute, quiet, or well-behaved, while boys are encouraged to be strong, fast, and fearless. That divide is not just cultural; it is damaging. It silently teaches girls to be spectators of their bodies rather than owners of them. It tells them their bodies are for looking at, not living in.

As her father, you must reject this mindset. Your daughter has the right to feel strong in her body. She has the right to run, climb, punch, kick, fall, sweat, and stand tall. Her body is not fragile. It is not a display piece. It is powerful, and it is hers. Your job is to help her realize that.

This starts with the way you talk to her. Praise her effort, not just the outcome. When she climbs the jungle gym, tell her how strong and determined she looked, not just how cute she was doing it. When she finishes a race, whether she wins or loses, highlight her grit and stamina. Shift the focus from appearance to ability. The world will do enough to teach her to care about being pretty; your role is to help her value being powerful.

It also starts with how you invest your time and attention. Take her outside. Encourage physical activity. Go on bike rides together, take weekend hikes, play catch in the yard, or sign up for a 5K you can train for side by side. The message is simple but profound: movement is normal, strength is expected, and her body is meant to *do* things. If you treat physical activity as part of everyday life, she will too.

If she's drawn to sports, support her fully. Show up for her games, learn the rules, cheer from the sidelines, and take her seriously. If she's not drawn to traditional sports, that's fine. There are countless other options. Rock climbing can teach problem-solving, bravery, and endurance. Dance, gymnastics, and even circus arts like aerial silks can cultivate a powerful relationship with movement and strength. Encourage her to try different things until something clicks.

You can even do these things with her. Join a father-daughter workout class, sign up for a beginner's obstacle course event, or practice self-defense drills together at home. Your participation reinforces the idea that strength is not only valuable but expected. And it becomes something you share, not something she has to figure out on her own.

Raising a physically strong daughter is about giving her permission to embrace who she already is. It's about showing her that her body is not a problem to fix but a tool to use. And when she learns that lesson early, she grows into a woman who walks through the world with presence, pride, and power.

From Playground to Practice: Build Her Up, Don't Hold Her Back

It starts small. A climb up the slide, a jump off the swing, a challenge to race you to the car. These may seem like everyday moments, but for your daughter, they are tests of courage, balance, and belief in her own ability. And how you respond matters. You can either fuel her confidence or plant doubt. You can say, "Be careful," or you can say, "You've got this." One protects her body, the other builds her spirit. She needs both, but too many girls grow up getting only the former.

From the moment she starts exploring the world, your daughter will push boundaries. She will want to run faster, climb higher, carry more, and try new things. Do not hold her back. Let her get messy, let her fall, let her try again. The scrapes, the stumbles, the missed catches, these are not failures. They are part of becoming someone who knows how to persevere. When you treat her physical efforts with seriousness and respect, she learns that her strength is real and worth developing.

This doesn't mean letting her run wild or ignoring danger; it means teaching her the difference between risk and recklessness. Show her how to spot what is truly unsafe, then encourage her to move forward when something just feels challenging. Let her struggle through the monkey bars, lift her own backpack, carry the groceries, shovel the driveway, or help move furniture. These may seem like small moments, but they build something huge: self-trust.

Enroll her in classes that push her physically while giving her a sense of control. Gymnastics, parkour, mixed martial arts, swimming, horseback riding, or strength and conditioning programs for kids can help her test and expand her limits. Martial arts, in particular, are a wise choice. Not only do they build strength, discipline, and focus, but they also teach specific tactics for protecting and defending oneself. As she grows older, you will not always be there to shield her from harm; she needs to know how to hold her ground, both physically and mentally. A daughter who knows how to fight back is not just safer; she is more confident, more self-assured, and less likely to walk through life feeling powerless.

But make sure whatever activity she chooses is fun, not forced. Ask her what excites her, what she wants to try, and then help make it happen. Sign her up, show up with her, and follow through. She'll feel stronger just knowing her dad believes she can handle it.

Model what it looks like to pursue physical strength without shame or hesitation. Let her see you working out, lifting weights, learning new physical skills, or pushing yourself in your own fitness goals. Share your wins and your struggles. Say things like, "That was tough, but I feel stronger today," or, "I didn't think I could do that, but I did." This gives her a living example of what strength looks like, not perfection, but perseverance.

Avoid the subtle ways adults tend to undermine girls' physical confidence. Don't flinch when she picks up something heavy. Don't call her "tiny but mighty" as if her strength is surprising. Don't joke about how she throws or climbs or runs. Instead, affirm her skill, her drive, her effort. Let her be powerful without needing to be dainty. Let her sweat, compete, and push herself without apology.

Fathers often say they want their daughters to be "strong," but too many unknowingly limit their daughters' physical experience of that word. Don't be one of them. Build her up. Let her test her edge. Give her room to try, to fail, and to rise again. When you do, you're not just helping her get stronger, you're helping her believe she already is.

Teaching Her to Take Up Space Without Apology

One of the greatest gifts you can give your daughter is the belief that she is allowed to take up space. Not just emotionally or intellectually, but physically as well. Too many girls grow up being told to shrink, to sit still, to stay quiet, to cross their legs, and to be "nice." The result is a generation of women who apologize for existing too loudly. You must teach your daughter the opposite. Her body is not something to hide or shrink, it is something to own.

Physical strength reinforces this truth in a way nothing else can. When she feels strong in her body, she is less likely to hunch her shoulders, to whisper when she speaks, or to let others walk over her, literally or figuratively. Strength teaches presence. It teaches posture. It gives her the right to walk into a room and know she belongs there.

Encourage her to move in ways that expand her space. Let her stretch, jump, run, and sprawl without shame. Make space for her at the dinner table, in the car, on the couch, not as a courtesy, but as her right. These little things add up. They shape the way she views her physical worth.

When she learns that she does not need to shrink to be accepted, she will be less likely to tolerate people who try to control or diminish her.

When she knows she is strong, she will walk through the world like she means it.

Teach Her to Be Her Own Protector

No matter how loving, watchful, or involved you are as a father, the truth remains: you will not always be there. You will not be there the first time she walks alone to her car in a dark parking lot, or the day someone crosses the line at a party, or the moment she feels her gut telling her something is off but isn't sure if she should speak up. In those moments, she cannot rely on you to protect her. She must rely on herself. And that means you must prepare her now, with the mindset, skills, and instincts of someone who can protect and defend herself when it matters most.

Teaching your daughter self-defense is not about making her paranoid. It is about making her *prepared*. Prepared to speak with authority. Prepared to trust her gut. Prepared to say no clearly and firmly, and to mean it. Prepared to fight back if she ever has to. A girl who is trained in self-defense doesn't live in fear; she lives with confidence. She walks into the world not as a victim-in-waiting, but as someone who knows her life and her safety are worth defending.

This training begins with awareness. Long before you take her to her first self-defense class, you can start teaching her how to observe her surroundings. Show her how to keep her head up and her phone down in public places. Discuss body language with her, explaining how predators often look for people who appear unsure, distracted, or afraid. Encourage her to walk with purpose, to make eye contact when needed, and to trust that uneasy feeling in her gut, even if she cannot explain it. Her instincts are a form of protection; your job is to help her honor them instead of overriding them out of politeness.

You must also give her permission to be loud. Girls are often taught to be quiet, to avoid conflict, and to keep the peace. But predators rely on silence and hesitation. Tell her directly: if someone makes you feel uncomfortable or unsafe, you do not have to be polite. You are allowed to say, "Back off." You are allowed to raise your voice. You are allowed to walk away without explanation. You are allowed to create a scene if it means getting safe. Drill that into her. Normalize it.

Enrolling her in a formal self-defense program can take this foundation even further. Look for classes that go beyond basic technique and focus on real-life scenarios. Programs like Krav Maga, RAD (Rape Aggression Defense), or women-centered personal protection courses teach more than punches and kicks. They teach mindset, boundary-setting, verbal assertiveness, and situational drills that simulate the kinds of encounters she might face in college, in public spaces, or on public transit. These classes are about giving her real tools, physical and mental, that she can use under pressure.

When she practices these skills in a safe environment, her fear response changes. She stops wondering what she would *do* in a dangerous situation because she's already trained for it. She doesn't freeze; she acts. And that mental shift can be the difference between vulnerability and survival. It can be the difference between a girl who panics and a girl who pushes back and gets to safety.

Support her through this process. If she feels nervous about taking a class, go with her. Train alongside her. Let her know she is not alone in learning how to protect herself. But also step back when needed and trust her to take it seriously. Self-defense isn't something you do *for* her; it's something you do *with* her until she owns it fully for herself.

You must also be mindful not to contradict the message at home. Do not scold her for speaking up, asserting her needs, or being "too intense." Do not joke about her being "too much" when she sets a boundary. If you want her to defend herself in the world, she has to be allowed to do it in her own home first. Respect her "no." Praise her when she uses her voice. Teach her that strength and safety are always more important than social niceties.

The truth is, you cannot control the world your daughter will face, but you can control how prepared she is to face it. You can raise her to believe that her safety matters. You can raise her to believe that her body is worth protecting. And you can raise her to know, deep in her bones, that she does not need to be rescued, because she has already learned to rescue herself.

Strong Body, Strong Mind: How Physical Confidence Builds Emotional Resilience

There is a direct line between how a girl feels in her body and how she handles life. Physical strength is more than just muscles or stamina; it's about self-trust, mental endurance, and emotional resilience. A daughter who believes in her physical ability is more likely to face setbacks with courage, recover from failure with perspective, and stand up for herself when it matters most. She knows that struggle is not something to fear, because she's already proven she can push through it.

Every time she lifts something heavier than she thought she could, or pushes through a workout she wanted to quit, she's training more than her body, she's training her mind. She is building discipline, confidence, and a relationship with effort. These qualities permeate every aspect of her life, including school, friendships, relationships, and ultimately, her career. When life gets hard, a strong girl doesn't immediately look for someone to rescue her. She takes a breath, steadies herself, and begins solving the problem. She knows she's been through hard things before, and she remembers what she's capable of.

As her father, you are instrumental in this. Your voice becomes part of her inner voice. When you cheer her on during physical challenges, when you tell her she's tough, when you celebrate her effort rather than her perfection, you are wiring her brain to associate discomfort with growth, not danger. You are helping her reframe what it means to struggle. Instead of seeing failure as a reflection of who she is, she learns to view it as a step toward improvement. Instead of quitting when things feel uncomfortable, she learns to lean in.

This matters even more during adolescence, when girls are particularly vulnerable to insecurity and comparison. The world will tell her that her worth is tied to how she looks. It will whisper that she needs to shrink, to smooth herself out, to fit in. But if you have helped her fall in love with what her body can *do*, she will be less likely to fall for those lies. She will stand in front of the mirror and see more than just flaws; she will see strength, movement, and resilience. That is the kind of body image that actually lasts.

Physical confidence also builds boundary-setting skills. A daughter who feels physically competent is less likely to tolerate unwanted touch, peer pressure, or intimidation. She knows she can say no, and she means it. She walks differently. She speaks differently. She is less afraid of confrontation because she has learned that strength does not mean aggression; it means certainty. It means holding your ground. That kind of self-assurance is a form of protection that goes far beyond any physical skill.

Encourage her to set physical goals. Not to lose weight or look a certain way, but to accomplish something: to get faster, lift more, master a skill, or build endurance. Let her see the results of her effort. Track her progress with her. Help her notice how she's getting stronger, how her recovery time is shorter, how her form is improving. Celebrate milestones not with rewards for her body, but with recognition of her strength.

Help her understand that strength and softness are not opposites. She can be kind and firm. She can be nurturing and powerful. She can cry and still be tough. Strength is not the absence of emotion; it's the ability to stay rooted while feeling deeply. When she begins to see strength this way, she will stop measuring herself against others and start measuring herself against who she was yesterday. That is where real confidence is born.

You will not be able to protect her from every challenge life throws at her. But you can and should give her the tools to face those challenges with grit and grace. You can help her build a body she trusts and a mind that does not fold under pressure. You can raise a daughter who knows, without a doubt, that she can handle herself in any room, on any field, or in any situation.

That kind of strength is not just physical; it is the foundation of the woman she will become.

Chapter Nine

Teach Her Real Love

Love will be one of the most defining forces in your daughter's life, shaping how she sees herself and what she believes she deserves from others. As her father, you are her first and most influential model of what love can feel like: safe, respectful, steady, and true. The lessons you teach her now will echo in every relationship she forms, especially the ones that challenge her self-worth. Help her recognize real love, reject control disguised as affection, and hold herself to a standard that never asks her to shrink in order to be loved.

Teach Her the Difference Between Love and Control

One of the most powerful lessons a father can teach his daughter about love is how to distinguish between genuine and insincere affection. Love and control are often confused, especially in a world where toxic relationships are romanticized in media, where jealousy is mistaken for passion, and where many young women are taught to prioritize keeping others happy over listening to their own instincts. As her father, you have a unique opportunity to plant the seeds of discernment early. You can show her what love is supposed to feel like: safe, steady, empowering, and free. And just as importantly, you can help her identify what love is not.

Love is not control. It is not manipulation. It is not possession or emotional dependency. It is not "if you loved me, you would..." or "you're nothing without me." These are the tools of fear and insecurity, not love. And the more clearly your daughter understands the difference, the stronger she will be and the less likely she will be to fall for a partner who uses control as a substitute for connection.

From the time she is young, your daughter is building a framework of what relationships look like. She sees how you handle conflict, how you listen, how you respect boundaries, and how you show affection. These small, everyday moments become her internal reference point. If she grows up with a father who respects her choices, honors her space, and makes her feel heard, she will learn to expect those same qualities from others. But if she learns that love means control, conditional affection, or emotional volatility, she may unknowingly repeat those patterns in her future relationships.

Many controlling relationships don't start out unhealthy. In fact, they often begin with excessive attention, flattery, or "protection." A controlling partner might say things like, "I just want to keep you safe," or "I worry about you all the time, that's why I get upset when you go out with your friends." At first glance, these statements can sound caring, even loving. But underneath them is a message that your daughter's autonomy is a threat, and that their love depends on her compliance. That is not love; it is fear in disguise.

As her father, you can help her develop an internal compass to recognize these warning signs. One way to do this is by naming and modeling *emotional safety*. Talk to her about how real love doesn't punish independence. Let her know that someone who loves her will want her to be free, to grow, to have her own friendships and dreams. Reassure her that love can withstand space, boundaries, and disagreements. The more she hears this from you, the more likely she is to recognize it when it's absent.

As she grows into adolescence and adulthood, the messages you've given her about love will compete with the ones she hears from peers, partners, and social media. These outside voices can be loud. Some may tell her that jealousy is proof of devotion. That intense emotional highs and lows are a normal part of life. That if a boy is possessive, it's only because he "loves her so much." These are dangerous lies. But they lose their power when your daughter already knows what love should feel like, because she felt it at home, from you.

You can reinforce this through simple, honest conversations. You don't have to lecture her about dating. Instead, ask open-ended questions. What do you think a healthy relationship looks like? What would be a red flag for you? How do you want to feel when you're with someone? These kinds of questions invite her to reflect and trust her instincts. They also give you a window into how she's thinking, and how you can guide her with gentle, firm truth.

It's also important to validate her feelings when she expresses discomfort about a friend, a teacher, a coach, or a crush. If she says someone made her uncomfortable, believe her. Do not downplay it. Teach her that her intuition is trustworthy. One of the earliest and most overlooked ways to affirm this is by respecting her bodily autonomy, especially around family and family friends. If she pulls back when asked to hug someone, even someone you trust like "Uncle Charlie," honor that boundary. Do not force her to hug or show affection when she is uncomfortable. It may seem harmless in the moment, but requiring her to ignore her own instincts in order to keep someone else comfortable sends a dangerous message: that her voice, her comfort, and her consent do not matter. When you affirm her boundaries and gut instincts, even in these small moments, you teach her not to second-guess herself in situations where something does not feel right. That kind of self-trust becomes a powerful defense against control later in life.

You can also use stories, from books, movies, or real life, to discuss the difference between love and control. Watch a show with her and ask what she thinks of a character's behavior. "Do you think that was respectful?" "How would you feel if someone said that to you?" These casual conversations can have a profound impact. They help her build a lens through which to critically evaluate relationships, rather than blindly accepting what appears "romantic" on the surface.

And perhaps most importantly, apologize when you make a mistake. If you speak over her, dismiss her feelings, or get too harsh, own up to it. Tell her you're sorry. Tell her you want to do better. When you do this, you're teaching her that love includes humility, repair, and accountability. She'll carry that standard with her into every relationship she has.

Your daughter deserves to know that love is not about control, it's about connection. It's not about owning someone, it's about honoring someone. The more clearly you model this, the more prepared she will be to spot the difference.

She may not always listen. She may roll her eyes. But she is absorbing your words and watching how you live. And when the time comes for her to choose whom to give her heart to, she'll reach for what feels familiar. Let that familiarity be the quiet confidence of being respected, the inner calm of being safe, and the unwavering knowledge that real love never needs to take away her freedom in order to prove its strength.

Teach her now, so she never confuses control with care.

Love Her Mother Well: The Relationship She Will Measure Against

Whether you're married to her mother, divorced, co-parenting, or never shared a household, your relationship with her mother is one of the most powerful and lasting messages your daughter will ever receive about love. While we briefly touched on this concept earlier in the book, it is so important that I wanted to circle back and explore it in more depth. The way you treat her mother, whether with kindness or contempt, sets the emotional tone for what she comes to believe about commitment, communication, respect, and emotional safety. Long after she forgets your words, she will remember how you treated her mother. That memory will quietly shape what she looks for in a partner and what she accepts.

Loving her mother well does not require a perfect relationship. In fact, it has little to do with outward displays of affection or grand romantic gestures. Loving her mother well means honoring her humanity. It means treating her with dignity in the presence of your daughter. It means never making your daughter choose sides, never using her as a pawn, and never modeling disrespect, even when tensions run high.

If you are still with her mother, your home becomes her first classroom on how relationships function. She watches how you argue. She observes how you apologize. She listens to how you speak when you are frustrated and how you show affection in the small, often unnoticed moments. The way you greet her mother at the end of the day, the way you respond to her needs, and the way you respect her opinions and contributions all become a mirror in your daughter's mind. If she sees a father who uplifts her mother, supports her dreams, and treats her with kindness even during disagreement, she will learn that love is steady and safe. She will expect to be treated with that same tenderness, and she will recognize when it is missing.

Even when the relationship has ended, the opportunity to teach your daughter what mature love looks like is still very much alive. In fact, parents who are divorced or separated often have an even greater opportunity to model respect under challenging circumstances. The way you speak about her mother when she is not around matters. The tone you use when discussing co-parenting decisions matters. A sigh of frustration, a sarcastic comment, or a dismissive joke may seem small to you, but your daughter deeply absorbs them. She is always listening; she is always watching.

Children internalize these messages in ways they may not always have the words to express. If your daughter hears you speak with contempt about her mother, she may begin to question parts of herself. She is made of both of you. When you criticize her mother, even indirectly, it can feel like a rejection of her identity. It may leave her feeling torn or confused, or burden her with the impossible task of trying to reconcile two people she loves. But when she hears you speak with respect and grace, even when it is difficult, she learns that maturity and character do not end when the relationship does. She learns that love, in its highest form, chooses dignity over bitterness.

Loving her mother well also teaches your daughter about emotional responsibility. It shows her that strong men do not blame, belittle, or shift accountability. They take ownership of their words and actions. They prioritize peace over pride. Even if your relationship with her mother is strained or painful, you can still model grace under pressure.

You can still show up calm, consistent, and with boundaries that are firm without being cruel.

This does not mean tolerating mistreatment or being passive in the face of ongoing conflict. Loving her mother well is not about pretending or denying reality. It is about handling what is difficult with honor. It means modeling disagreement in a way that is not demeaning. It means knowing when to walk away from an argument, how to apologize sincerely, and how to repair the damage after a rupture has occurred. These moments of emotional maturity are among the most powerful forms of love your daughter will ever experience.

In healthy, intact marriages, loving her mother well often looks like the quiet, everyday moments of partnership. It is sharing responsibilities without keeping score. It is noticing when she is tired and stepping in without being asked. It is validating her voice, celebrating her strengths, and being generous with appreciation. Your daughter is watching. When she sees her father valuing her mother's intelligence, treating her with tenderness, and investing in the well-being of the family, she learns that love is an action. It is consistent. It is respectful.

If you are in a new relationship, whether remarried or dating, how you speak about your daughter's mother still matters. Your new partner may be a part of her life, but your daughter only has one mother. Honor that bond. Do not make jokes at her mother's expense, even in private. Do not compare. Do not pit them against each other. Your ability to treat her mother with respect, even in complex situations, reinforces your daughter's sense of emotional stability and teaches her what true character looks like.

Not every parenting situation is healthy or equal. Some relationships involve high conflict, emotional abuse, or unsafe dynamics. In such cases, loving her mother well may mean maintaining a distance while using neutral language. It may mean setting boundaries for yourself and your daughter while still affirming that she has the right to love both of her parents. Do not weaponize your pain. Do not overshare. Your daughter is not your confidant. She is your child. She deserves to grow up free from guilt, shame, or the burden of emotional triangulation.

When a father shows love, respect, or restraint toward his daughter's mother, he is doing more than just modeling good behavior; he is shaping her worldview. He is teaching her that love does not require humiliation. That strength is not measured by domination. That real men do not weaponize silence or blame. They communicate. They take responsibility. They protect what matters, even when it is hard.

Your relationship with her mother is the backdrop against which your daughter will measure every future relationship she has. Let that backdrop be one of honor, not hostility; of patience, not pettiness; of care, not control. In time, she will forget specific conversations and passing moments, but she will not forget how you made her feel, or how you made her mother feel.

And when she stands on the threshold of love, whether choosing a partner, setting a boundary, or walking away from someone who does not treat her right, your influence will echo in the quiet of her decisions. Let that influence say, without needing to be spoken: Love is kind. Love is respectful. Love is safe.

Loving her mother well may be one of the most enduring ways you ever teach your daughter what real love looks like.

Show Her What Strength Really Looks Like

In a world that often confuses control with confidence and aggression with authority, one of the most powerful lessons a father can teach his daughter is what real strength truly looks like. As she grows, your example will help her distinguish between false strength, the kind that dominates, intimidates, or silences, and true strength, which is rooted in self-control, compassion, and integrity. This difference matters deeply because it shapes the kind of strength she will seek in others and cultivate in herself.

Your daughter is constantly exposed to conflicting messages about strength. In many stories, the "strong man" is the one who never cries, never apologizes, and never backs down. He always has the last word, always controls the room, and always gets his way. This version of masculinity is shallow and performative. It thrives on dominance, not connection. And if this is what she comes to associate with strength, she may begin to believe that love must come with intimidation, or that kindness is weakness.

You have the power to rewrite that script. You can show her that strength is not about overpowering others, but about mastering yourself. True strength is quiet, not loud; steady, not reactive; protective, not possessive. It shows up when it matters most, in how you handle stress, how you respond to failure, how you treat those with less power than you, and how you act when no one is watching.

One of the clearest ways to model this is through emotional regulation. When you are angry, do you lash out or do you pause? When you are disappointed, do you withdraw or do you communicate? Your daughter is watching. When she sees you handle frustration without losing your temper, she learns that strength is not about unleashing rage but about choosing calm. When she sees you take responsibility for your actions, she learns that real men do not blame others; they own their impact.

Apologizing is one of the most courageous acts of strength you can demonstrate. Many men were never taught how to say "I'm sorry" with sincerity, especially to their children. But when you do, you are not showing weakness; you are showing humility and accountability. You are teaching her that strength is not found in always being right, but in being willing to repair what was hurt. A father who can apologize is a father who teaches his daughter that love is safe, that conflict can be resolved, and that mistakes do not make someone unlovable.

Your daughter also learns strength by watching how you treat others, particularly those who are vulnerable. Do you show kindness to strangers? Do you speak respectfully to people in service roles? Do you offer help without expecting praise? These everyday choices shape her understanding of what character looks like. When she sees her father use his strength to protect, support, and uplift others, she internalizes that strength should never be used to diminish or intimidate.

Physical presence is another dimension of strength, and it matters, but it is not the full picture. Being strong for your daughter means more than protecting her from danger. It means being emotionally present, mentally engaged, and spiritually grounded. It means showing up when it would be easier to withdraw. It means holding space for her feelings without needing to fix them or explain them away. Your ability to remain steady while she feels messy or overwhelmed teaches her that she is safe in her emotions, and that she deserves a partner who can be steady too.

True strength also includes setting boundaries, not only for her, but for yourself. A strong father knows how to say no without anger, how to enforce rules with compassion, and how to prioritize his family even when it costs him time, comfort, or ego. When you uphold your values with quiet confidence, you teach her that strength means standing firm without becoming rigid or harsh. She learns that love can be both soft and strong, flexible and grounded.

That is why it is so important that your strength never comes at the cost of her dignity, her voice, or her autonomy. Do not confuse obedience with connection. Your goal is not to raise a daughter who fears your disapproval, but one who trusts your presence. Strength that relies on fear or control is fragile; it eventually breaks down. However, strength built on love, trust, and presence will hold fast even when life becomes difficult.

Let her see you handle failure with grace. Let her see you struggle and keep going. Let her see you cry and still stand tall. These moments of honest vulnerability are not signs that you are falling apart; they are signs that you are fully human. And when she sees that humanity in you, she will permit herself to embrace her own.

She will grow up in a world that tells her she must be smaller, quieter, or more agreeable in order to be accepted. But if she has seen real strength in you, she will know that strength is not about fitting in; it is about standing tall in who you are. She will know that strength is not found in someone who needs to control her, but in someone who honors her.

And if she ever finds herself doubting her worth, trying to win someone's approval, or excusing someone's mistreatment, she will have your example to return to. She will remember how you treated her. She will remember how you showed up, how you listened, how you loved her mother, how you handled conflict, and how you remained calm in the storm.

That is what real strength looks like. Not force. Not volume. Not control. But steady, grounded, present love.

And when she sees it in you, she will learn to expect nothing less from the world around her.

Set the Standard So She Never Settles

One of the greatest gifts a father can give his daughter is a deep and unwavering belief in her worth. When a daughter knows her value, she is far less likely to accept relationships that diminish her, harm her, or force her to shrink herself in order to be loved. She will not confuse affection with control, intensity with intimacy, or validation with love. She will know the difference because she has seen the real thing, modeled by you.

Setting the standard means more than telling her she deserves the best. It means showing her what healthy, respectful love actually looks like in real life. It means teaching her, through both word and action, that she never has to earn someone's approval by abandoning parts of herself. And it means making sure she knows that the love she accepts from others should always reflect the love you have consistently given to her; steady, respectful, safe, and whole.

Fathers set the standard in both obvious and subtle ways. The way you treat her sets the bar for how she expects others to treat her. If you listen when she speaks, she will expect to be heard. If you respect her emotions, she will expect to be respected. If you show up when it matters, she will believe she is worthy of someone who stays. These daily moments, while small on the surface, become the foundation of her self-concept.

When you speak to her with kindness, even when correcting her, you teach her that love and firmness can coexist. When you ask her how she feels and listen without interrupting, you teach her that her voice is valued and matters. When you show pride in her efforts rather than just her achievements, you teach her that she is valued for who she is, not for what she accomplishes. These lessons shape her identity. And a daughter who knows her identity will not settle for love that erodes it.

But this standard-setting also requires you to speak directly about relationships, especially as she enters adolescence and young adulthood. You cannot assume she will figure it out on her own, or that she will just know what to avoid. She needs you to be explicit. Talk to her about red flags: controlling behavior, possessiveness, disrespect, and emotional volatility. Talk to her about green flags: consistency, kindness, emotional safety, shared values. Let her know that it is not dramatic or harsh to walk away from someone who makes her feel small; it is an act of strength.

Affirm her instincts. If something feels wrong to her, it probably is. Encourage her to trust her gut, to name discomfort, to speak up when something does not feel right. These are tools of discernment, and she will need them long before she is ever in a serious relationship. The earlier you teach her to recognize what healthy love looks like, the better able she will be to walk away from what is not.

Part of helping her build high standards also includes guiding her through the realities of loneliness, doubt, and pressure. There may come a time when she feels tempted to stay in a relationship simply because it is familiar, because all her friends are in one, or because she fears being alone. These moments are pivotal. They are when the foundation you have laid will matter most. Your voice, if it has been consistent and loving, will echo in her mind and remind her that she is never truly alone, that she is already enough, and that no relationship is worth losing herself over.

It is also crucial that you teach her that love is not something she must hustle for. She does not need to perform, prove, or earn her way into being loved. If she grows up hearing conditional messages: "I love you when you behave," "You make me proud when you achieve," "I'm disappointed in you because you're emotional," she may come to believe that love is always dependent on performance. That belief is the first step toward settling. She will tolerate partners who love her only when she is pleasing, only when she is agreeable, only when she is perfect.

To prevent this, you must be the one who sees her clearly and loves her anyway. You must be the one who reminds her that love is a place of safety, not pressure. You must tell her she is worthy, even when she is struggling. You must love her when she fails, when she is moody, when she doubts herself, because that is when your love matters most. That is when it becomes the standard she will carry with her into every relationship she forms.

Model for her what it looks like to walk away from what does not honor you. This could mean ending toxic friendships, setting boundaries with family members, or refusing to tolerate disrespect in your own life. Let her see that real men do not tolerate harmful behavior, even when it is uncomfortable to confront. When she sees you hold boundaries with integrity, she learns that strength is not about keeping the peace at any cost; it is about protecting what matters.

Remind her, often, that she never has to settle out of fear. Fear of being alone. Fear of disappointing someone. Fear of not finding someone else. Love is not a race. It is not a reward for being likable or perfect. It is something she is already worthy of, simply because she exists.

And when that day comes, whether she is in high school, college, or well into adulthood, when she brings someone home and looks to you, consciously or not, for affirmation, she will compare this person to the man who first taught her what love looks like. She will measure them against the standard you set. Not because you are the final authority, but because your presence in her life built the very foundation upon which she stands.

That is the power of fatherhood. To set a standard so high, so loving, so steady, that anything less becomes immediately obvious.

Not every daughter will listen to your advice the first time. Some may learn through hard experiences. But when your standard has been grounded in love, respect, and truth, she will always have something to come back to. A memory of what it felt like to be seen, cherished, and valued without having to shrink herself to fit someone else's mold.

Let her carry that into the world. Let her expect love that strengthens, not weakens. Love that frees, not binds. Love that lifts, not drains.

Set the standard, and she will know what it feels like to never settle.

Chapter Ten

Raising a Daughter of Character

We all want our daughters to grow into women who are strong, capable, and respected. But real strength is not just about confidence or ambition, it is rooted in character. The way she works, the values she holds, and the choices she makes when no one is watching will shape her future far more than talent or charm ever could. As her father, you are the one who teaches her what it means to live with integrity, to take pride in her efforts, and to lead herself with clarity and conviction.

Give Her a Strong Work Ethic

Your daughter may have natural gifts; she may be artistic, athletic, intuitive, or sharp-witted. But if she never learns how to work hard, to persevere, to push through when things are difficult or dull, those talents will never take her where they could. Talent may open the door, but it is work ethic that keeps it open. One of the most important things you can teach your daughter is that her future will not be built solely on ability; it will be shaped by how she behaves when no one is watching, how she perseveres when things are challenging, and how she responds to setbacks.

In a world obsessed with quick wins and overnight success, it is easy for a child to believe that effort is optional. Social media glorifies highlight reels and filters out the process. What your daughter needs most is a father who shows her that greatness is not glamorous; it is built in small, consistent, often invisible steps. You teach her this not just by telling her to try hard, but by modeling it in your own life. She is watching how you handle challenges. She is noticing whether you give up or stick with things when they are inconvenient, tedious, or difficult. She hears how you talk about your work, your goals, your disappointments. She learns from how you carry yourself.

Work ethic is not about perfection. It is about mindset. When you praise her for her effort, her attitude, and her persistence rather than just her outcomes, you teach her to find pride in the process. If she brings home a good grade, praise the effort she put into studying. If she loses a game, acknowledge the way she showed up and kept playing. If she takes on something new and struggles, let her know how proud you are that she was willing to try. These messages matter. They teach her that her worth is not measured solely by success, but by how she commits, how she endures, and how she grows.

Failure is one of the best teachers she will ever have; if she is allowed to learn from it. Resist the urge to rescue her from every mistake or disappointment. Let her fall, gently, and help her reflect on what she learned. When she sees that failure is not the end but a step forward, she becomes more resilient. She stops avoiding hard things out of fear. She stops needing everything to be perfect. And she begins to understand that confidence is not the absence of failure, but the result of walking through it and coming out stronger.

Chores, schoolwork, practice, and even everyday responsibilities are all opportunities to shape her character. They are not punishments; they are preparation. When you teach her to follow through on commitments, to do things well even when they are tedious, and to take responsibility without complaining, you are preparing her for a life of success. These habits form the structure she will lean on when life gets overwhelming. They help her develop grit, reliability, and pride in her own integrity.

That does not mean pushing her beyond what is developmentally appropriate or expecting perfection from her. It means holding her to a standard that stretches her. It means not letting her quit the first time something gets hard. It means expecting her to contribute to the household, not because she owes you, but because responsibility is part of being a member of a family. It means encouraging her to do things for herself: make her bed, manage her schedule, and recover from mistakes. Because every time she masters something on her own, she becomes more confident in her ability to meet life head-on.

Your words carry weight. When she hears you say things like, "I am proud of how hard you worked," or "That was a tough situation and you handled it with maturity," you are shaping the way she sees herself. You are helping her internalize a voice that says, "I can do hard things. I can keep going. I can figure it out." That inner voice will be there when you are not. It will speak to her when she faces a challenge, a temptation, or a setback. Make sure it is a voice that encourages her to rise, not retreat.

Work ethic also teaches her to take pride in things that are not immediately rewarded. It helps her develop discipline in a world that tempts her to cut corners and opt for the easy way. When you show her that integrity means doing the right thing even when no one is watching, she starts to understand that her reputation is not built in moments of recognition; it is built in what she does every day. She learns that success is earned, not given. And that the satisfaction of doing something well is worth far more than empty praise.

There will be moments when she wants to give up. Moments when things feel too hard, too slow, or too uncertain. In those moments, she needs a father who reminds her of who she is and what she is capable of. Not a father who solves everything for her, but one who walks beside her and believes in her ability to endure. She needs to know that you see her strength, even when she is tired. That you are not afraid of her struggle. That you respect the way she keeps trying.

As she grows older, these lessons will serve her well in every area of life, including school, relationships, career, and parenting. She will know how to keep going when others give up. She will know how to stay grounded when life does not give instant results. She will know how to recover from failure with grace and determination. And she will know that success is not just about reaching the top, but about becoming the kind of woman who earns her place through effort, character, and courage.

By teaching her the value of hard work, you are giving her something far more lasting than any praise or protection can offer. You are giving her the tools to build her own life. And in the process, you are also teaching her something about you, that you are a man who values effort, resilience, and doing what is right. That you are not just raising a daughter, but raising a strong, capable, and grounded young woman who knows how to rise on her own.

Because in the end, your example becomes her expectation. When you show up with integrity, follow through with discipline, and keep trying even when things are challenging, you are demonstrating what it means to work with heart. And that is the kind of strength she will carry into the world, not just because you told her to, but because she saw it in you.

Do the Right Thing, Even When No One Is Watching

What truly defines a person is not how they behave when others are watching, but how they act when no one is there to see. This truth applies to adults, and it applies just as powerfully to children. Your daughter is growing up in a world where image often matters more than integrity, where being liked can feel more important than being right, and where shortcuts are often rewarded more visibly than doing things the hard, honest way. That is why teaching her to live by a moral compass is one of the most crucial aspects of your role as her father.

Doing the right thing, even when it is inconvenient, uncomfortable, or unnoticed, is the foundation of character. It is also one of the clearest signs of inner strength. Your daughter will face moments when she must decide whether to speak up or remain silent, whether to include someone or conform to the crowd, and whether to tell the truth or protect her image. In those moments, she will draw not just from what you have taught her, but from what she has seen you live out.

You cannot expect her to develop integrity if she never sees it in action. She learns it when she watches you admit a mistake instead of making excuses. She learns it when you return money that was given to you by accident, when you keep your word even though it would be easier not to, and when you treat people with respect regardless of what they can do for you. These moments do not need a spotlight. In fact, their power lies in their quietness. They are absorbed into her value system in real-time, often without a single word being exchanged.

Fathers often underestimate the quiet ways their daughters are shaped. A simple act, apologizing sincerely, holding firm to your principles, or standing up for someone who is being mistreated, becomes a lesson that will live with her forever. These are the kinds of actions that teach her what it looks like to live with courage and compassion. These are the things she will carry into classrooms, friendships, relationships, and eventually into the kind of adult she becomes.

But modeling is only part of the equation. She also needs opportunities to practice making value-based decisions for herself. When you involve her in conversations about fairness, honesty, loyalty, and responsibility, you teach her how to think through moral dilemmas. Ask her questions that matter: "What do you think is the right thing to do?" "Why do you think this matters?" "How do you feel about what just happened?" These kinds of conversations help her build her internal compass and trust her own voice.

Let her wrestle with difficult questions, and resist the urge to give her all the answers. Instead, guide her gently as she learns to evaluate situations through the lens of values. There will be times when she gets it wrong. That is not a failure; it is a necessary part of moral development. When you help her reflect, learn, and try again, you are giving her a safe space to become the kind of person who does the right thing because it is right, not because someone is watching.

It is also important to discuss integrity openly, even when others do not demonstrate it. When your daughter sees someone lie, cheat, or manipulate and still succeed, she may question the point of doing the right thing. That is a natural reaction, especially in a culture that often rewards performance over principle. This is when your guidance matters most. Help her see that real peace comes from a clean conscience.

Help her understand that her character will outlast every temporary win or superficial praise. Teach her that sleeping well at night is far more valuable than being applauded by the crowd.

There is strength in restraint. There is power in walking away from gossip, in refusing to take part in cruelty, in owning up to a mistake before someone finds out. These are not small things. These are acts of courage, and they deserve to be honored. When your daughter sees that you notice and respect these choices in others, she learns to value them in herself. When you commend her not just for achievements, but for choosing kindness or honesty in difficult moments, you are reinforcing what truly matters.

And when she makes a mistake, which she inevitably will, your response is crucial. If she tells the truth and faces consequences, let her see that you value her integrity more than her perfection. If she apologizes, let her feel your respect for her humility. These moments of failure are sacred ground. They are opportunities to deepen her sense of identity and morality. They are where trust is built and where shame can be replaced with growth and development.

Doing the right thing is not always the easiest path to follow. It often comes with resistance, judgment, or being misunderstood. Your daughter needs to know that she can choose what is right without losing your approval. She needs to know that you are not raising her to be liked by everyone; you are raising her to be proud of who she is when she looks in the mirror.

Help her understand that being good is not about being perfect. It is about aligning her actions with her values, about choosing to stand tall when it would be easier to shrink, about speaking truth when silence feels safer. This is what it means to have a moral compass. And it begins with you.

Every small decision you make to uphold your values becomes part of her internal map. Every time you choose kindness over ego, honesty over image, or responsibility over convenience, you are showing her what true strength looks like. You are giving her something more valuable than popularity or approval; you are giving her the courage to live with integrity.

And in doing so, you are helping her become a young woman who knows who she is, who respects herself, and who does not compromise what matters most just to fit in. That is the kind of daughter who will walk into the world with quiet confidence. That is the kind of daughter who leads not just with her voice, but with her example. And it begins with a father who shows her, every day, that character counts.

Your Values Are Her Compass

Every daughter will eventually face moments in life where she is unsure which direction to take. The world will offer her loud opinions, conflicting messages, and pressures that pull her in opposite directions. In those moments, she will reach for something steady, something that tells her who she is and what kind of life she wants to live. That something is her internal compass, and much of it is shaped by the values you live out in front of her.

Your values become her orientation. The way you treat people, the way you handle adversity, and the way you show up when it matters are all teaching tools. She is not just listening to what you say; she is absorbing what you prioritize. If you claim to value honesty, but regularly bend the truth, she will learn that integrity is not always rigid. If you emphasize kindness, but speak harshly when you are angry, she will learn that empathy has limits. If you value responsibility but avoid accountability when things go wrong, she will internalize that rules are for other people. The values you embody, consistently, quietly, and especially when it is hard, are the ones she will carry forward.

Values are not just lofty ideals; they are the foundation of a life well lived. They influence how she treats others, how she allows herself to be treated, and how she makes difficult decisions. When you demonstrate values like humility, patience, courage, generosity, and self-control, you provide her with examples she can draw upon when her own character is tested. She may not copy every choice you make, but she will hold onto the principles you showed her matter most.

One of the most effective ways to pass on your values is through your response to real-life situations. When someone is rude to you, do you retaliate or respond with grace? When you make a mistake, do you blame others or own it with humility? When someone else succeeds, do you celebrate their success or feel a sense of competition? These small moments may feel inconsequential, but they are formative. Your daughter watches how you live your values, not just when things are easy, but especially when they are not.

Talk about your values openly. Tell her why you made a decision, even if it was unpopular. Tell her about a time you struggled to do the right thing, and what helped you choose well. Let her see that living by your values is not always convenient, but it is always worth it. These conversations give her insight not only into your principles, but into your humanity. They teach her that values are not abstract rules; they are lived choices that require practice, reflection, and courage.

She also needs to feel that your values include her. When you emphasize empathy, make space for her feelings. When you value respect, show her what it looks like to respect her voice and boundaries. When you talk about responsibility, let her see that you trust her with age-appropriate responsibilities. The more she sees your values shaping how you treat her, the more she will understand that they are not just ideas; they are a way of being.

Spirituality or faith, if present in your life, can be another grounding force. Whether you follow a specific tradition or hold spiritual beliefs about compassion, justice, or purpose, your daughter will take note of how your beliefs shape your actions. When she sees that your values are rooted in something deeper than opinion or convenience, she will begin to consider what she wants her own foundation to be. Do not force belief upon her; instead, model it. Let her see the peace, the strength, and the guidance that your spiritual life brings you, and invite her into conversations that help her explore what she believes for herself.

Culture, family traditions, and generational stories also play a decisive role in shaping values. Tell her where your values came from, who taught you, who influenced you, and what moments in your life shaped what you now believe is important. Sharing stories about your parents, your struggles, and your growth creates a sense of legacy. It helps her see that values are not just rules to follow; they are a living inheritance, something passed down from one generation to the next, and something she will one day pass on as well.

Let her also see your values in action within your relationships. How you speak to your partner, how you treat people who serve you, how you handle differences with others, all of these moments reveal what you value. If you treat others with compassion, even when you disagree, she will learn that strength and kindness can coexist. If you honor commitments and show up when you say you will, she will learn that your word means something. These are the lessons that build her compass.

And when her own values begin to emerge, welcome them. She may not always agree with you, and that is a sign of her growing independence. Ask her what matters most to her. Invite her to reflect on why she feels strongly about certain issues. Let her know that developing her own values is not rebellion; it is a sign of growth. Your job is not to control her moral outlook, but to guide her toward becoming a person who lives with conviction and integrity.

In a world that constantly tries to pull her away from herself, your values will be a lighthouse. They will be what she returns to when she feels lost, what she leans on when she is pressured to compromise, and what she uses to steady herself when life becomes uncertain. She may not remember every rule you set or every speech you gave, but she will remember the way you lived.

Ultimately, what you model is what she will measure against. Your values, if they are strong, lived, and rooted in love, will become hers. And they will guide her through friendships, love, work, loss, temptation, and triumph. You are not just influencing how she behaves. You are helping shape who she becomes.

And when she chooses honesty over ease, compassion over cruelty, or courage over comfort, you will know it was not by chance. It was because her morals and value system were formed by watching you.

Raising a Daughter Who Can Lead Herself

The ultimate goal of parenting is not control; it is leadership. And the most powerful kind of leadership is the kind that eventually steps back and watches someone thrive on their own. As a father, you are not raising a girl to remain dependent on your voice. You are raising a young woman who can trust her own. Teaching your daughter to develop a strong work ethic and moral compass is not about managing her every move; it is about teaching her to lead herself with clarity, strength, and conviction.

Leadership begins with self-awareness. Your daughter needs to know who she is apart from external labels or expectations. That sense of identity starts with you. The way you speak to her, the way you respond to her struggles, the way you reflect back her strengths, all of it forms the foundation of how she sees herself. When you affirm her for qualities like courage, kindness, discipline, and thoughtfulness, rather than just performance or appearance, you help her build a self-image that is grounded and whole.

Let her make choices. Let her wrestle with decisions, consider consequences, and listen to her instincts. The more ownership she has over her life, the more confident she becomes in her ability to direct it. This does not mean stepping away entirely; it means stepping back just enough to let her practice navigating with the tools you have given her. Be her advisor, not her controller. Be the steady voice she knows she can come to, but not the one who always takes over.

Teach her that leadership is not about control or popularity. It is about living with purpose, treating others with dignity, and having the courage to stand alone when necessary. Whether she leads a team, a family, a community, or simply her own life, she will need the ability to listen deeply, think critically, and act with integrity. These traits are not developed overnight. They are cultivated through everyday experiences where she learns to reflect, take responsibility, and grow from mistakes.

Let her experience struggle. Let her face frustration, failure, and moments of discomfort. These are not signs of weakness; they are invitations to build resilience. When she has to work hard for something, when she feels the sting of consequences, when she must recover from a misstep, she learns what she is made of. Do not steal those moments from her in an effort to protect her. Instead, be present in them. Encourage her to keep going. Remind her that struggle does not define her; it strengthens her.

Leadership also requires emotional intelligence. Help her name her feelings. Teach her to pause before reacting, to listen before judging, and to speak with both strength and grace. The more she understands her own emotions, the more effectively she can lead herself and connect with others. Emotional regulation is not just a personal skill; it is a leadership tool. It allows her to respond to life thoughtfully, rather than impulsively.

Your daughter will face moments when it is tempting to follow others, to stay silent when she disagrees, or to shrink herself to avoid rejection. In those moments, her ability to lead herself will be tested. That is why it is so important to help her develop internal standards. When she knows what she believes, what she values, and what she expects from herself and others, she will not be easily swayed. She will be able to make hard decisions with clarity and confidence.

Model that kind of self-leadership in your own life. Let her see you make thoughtful decisions, own your mistakes, and stay true to your values even when it is hard. When she sees you lead yourself with humility and strength, she learns that she can do the same. Let her watch you say no when something does not align with your priorities. Let her hear you say, "I was wrong," and mean it. Let her witness your growth. These examples give her permission to lead with integrity and authenticity.

Encourage her to think critically. Ask her open-ended questions. Invite her opinion on real-world issues. Help her see that her voice matters, not because she is always right, but because her perspective is valuable. When you listen to her with genuine interest, you empower her to trust her own mind. And when you challenge her gently to consider different viewpoints, you strengthen her ability to lead with thoughtfulness rather than impulse.

Remind her that leadership also means service. It is not about being above others; it is about lifting them up. Teach her to use her influence for good, to advocate for the vulnerable, to speak up when something is wrong, and to reach back for others once she has moved forward. The strongest leaders are those who lead from within, who do not rely on titles or praise, but who live from a deep and steady sense of purpose.

You will not always be there to guide her. One day, she will face a crossroads with no one watching. No applause, no reassurance, no step-by-step instructions. In that moment, she will lean on the strength she has cultivated, the values she has internalized, and the example she saw in you. She will take a breath, feel the weight of her own conscience, and choose the path that reflects who she is. And that choice will not be a fluke. It will be the fruit of everything you have poured into her.

Because in the end, that is what you are doing: raising a daughter who does not just follow rules, but who leads herself with confidence and clarity. A daughter who understands that strength comes from within, that responsibility is a privilege, and that character always outlasts charm. You are raising a daughter who will not need constant direction because you have given her something better: your example, your presence, and your unwavering belief in her.

She will carry those gifts into every room she enters. She will speak with calm conviction. She will show up when others hesitate. She will lead herself with purpose, with courage, and with heart.

And you will know that you helped build that. You raised a daughter who does not follow the crowd because you taught her to trust her moral values. You raised a daughter who stands tall because you showed her how. You raised a daughter who leads from within because you led her well.

Chapter Eleven

Teach Your Daughter About Sex and Consent

There are few conversations more uncomfortable for a parent than the one about sex. It is easy to hesitate, hoping that school will cover it or that she will somehow figure it out on her own when the time comes. But the truth is that if you do not talk to her, someone else will; and that someone may not have her best interest at heart. Whether it is through peers, the internet, or the culture around her, she will be exposed to messages about sex, relationships, and her body. The question is not whether she will learn it, but from whom she will learn it.

As her father, your voice matters more than you may realize. You do not have to explain every detail, but you do need to ensure she knows she can come to you, that you will answer her honestly, and that her body, boundaries, and voice are always hers. Talking to her about sex and consent is about her physical safety, her emotional security, confidence, and dignity. It is about raising a daughter who understands that her body is her own, that no one has the right to touch her without clear and enthusiastic permission, and that she never has to sacrifice her comfort to keep someone else happy.

Consent is the foundation of every healthy relationship. It means freely given, informed, enthusiastic, and reversible permission. It is not silence. It is not fear. It is not pressure. It is not owed, expected, or assumed. Consent means she is fully on board, emotionally, physically, mentally, and that she has every right to change her mind at any point.

You need to be the one who teaches her that. Because if you do not, someone else will. And the voices that fill that space might not teach her respect or self-protection. They might teach her to stay quiet to keep the peace, to sacrifice her comfort for approval, or to confuse love with obligation.

Start when she is young. Teaching consent does not begin with a serious talk about sex. It starts the moment you show her that her body is hers. When she says "no," take her seriously. Do not make her hug a family friend if she does not want to. Do not tell her to smile when she is uncomfortable. Respect her boundaries, even when they seem small. These moments send a powerful message: your body is yours, and you have the right to decide what happens to it.

As she gets older, begin to name what consent really looks like. It is not a one-time agreement. It is an ongoing conversation. It can be withdrawn at any time. It must be mutual and without manipulation. Teach her the difference between consent and compliance. Compliance is when someone says yes because they are scared, confused, or pressured. Consent, real consent, feels safe and clear and chosen.

Talk to her about what pressure can look like, because it does not always look like force. Sometimes it looks like guilt. Sometimes it looks like persistence. Sometimes it looks like someone ignoring her hesitation or trying to convince her that she is being too sensitive. She needs to know that if she ever feels uncomfortable, she is allowed to say no. And she is allowed to leave. She does not owe anyone an explanation.

Help her recognize red flags. If someone refuses to take no for an answer, that is not romantic; it is controlling. If someone makes her feel guilty for setting boundaries, that is not love; it is manipulation. If someone crosses a boundary once, they are more likely to do it again. Teach her to trust her instincts. If something feels off, it probably is.

Let her know that **real respect sounds like:**

- "Are you okay with this?"

- "Do you want to keep going?"

- "Tell me what you're comfortable with."

And if those questions are not being asked, she should not be staying.

It is also essential that she knows consent applies to **every kind of physical contact,** not just sex. Touching her hair, grabbing her hand, pulling her into a hug; if she does not want it, she is allowed to say no. If someone touches her in a way she does not like, she is allowed to speak up, move away, and protect her space. This builds both physical and emotional boundaries.

You must also give her language. Phrases like:

- "That makes me uncomfortable."

- "I'm not okay with that."

- "Please don't touch me."

- "No, I don't want to."

Simple, direct words that are clear and firm. The earlier she becomes comfortable using them, the more naturally they will come to her when she needs them.

And just as important: teach her how to receive someone else's no. If a friend says they do not want a hug, if a peer says they need space, she should honor that without offense. Consent is not just about protecting herself; it is about respecting others, too.

Consent education is not one talk. It is a series of conversations that evolve as she grows. Let her know she can come to you at any time with questions, with confusion, with fear. Let her know you will not shame her, interrogate her, or make her feel small. What she needs from you is safety, not judgment. Support, not punishment. If she is hurt, confused, or in trouble, she needs to know your love is not conditional.

You are protecting her body and you are protecting her belief that she has the right to be safe. You are protecting her sense of ownership over her own life. You are protecting her from a culture that often blurs lines and confuses consent with performance. You are giving her a voice that will speak loudly when others try to silence it.

And perhaps most importantly, you are showing her what it means to be respected. When you treat her with dignity, when you honor her words, when you give her space to feel in control of her body, you are giving her the blueprint. You are setting the standard she will carry with her.

Because one day she will be in a room with someone who does not respect her. And when that moment comes, you want your voice in her head. Not one that says, "Be nice," or "Don't make it awkward," or "Maybe it's not a big deal." You want your voice to say, "You are allowed to say no. You are allowed to leave. You are allowed to put yourself first."

And that voice, the one you planted with consistency and care, might be the one that keeps her safe.

Conclusion

The Legacy You Leave Behind

Being a father is not always easy. Some days you will question yourself, wonder if you are getting through, or feel the weight of your own mistakes. But none of that takes away from the impact you are making. Because showing up, trying again, and loving her through it all—that is what lasts.

You are not just influencing her childhood. You are shaping the woman she will grow into. The way she holds herself in the world. The way she handles adversity. The way she trusts, the way she leads, the way she loves. She will carry your words and your silence, your actions and your absence. Every part of how you father her becomes part of how she sees herself.

And the beauty is, you do not have to get it all right. You just have to stay in it. Stay present. Stay open. Stay committed to the long work of loving her well. Because fatherhood is not about grand performances; it is about quiet consistency. The hugs she did not ask for but needed. The boundaries that felt hard but kept her safe. The moments when you listened without trying to fix. These are the gifts that build her strength from the inside out.

Someday she will tell stories about her childhood. And in those stories, she will name what mattered. Not the things you bought her, but the way you made her feel. Not how perfect you were, but how steady you remained. She will remember that she was loved, deeply and without condition. That she mattered to her father. That he saw her, believed in her, and stood beside her.

That is the kind of father you have the power to be. And that is the kind of love that will live on long after she's grown.

References

American Psychological Association. (n.d.). *Resilience guide for parents and teachers*. https://www.apa.org/topics/resilience/guide-parents-teachers

Awakened Path Counseling. (n.d.). *The power of ritual: How simple family traditions can support emotional well-being in children*. https://www.awakenedpathcounseling.com/the-power-of-ritual-how-simple-family-traditions-can-support-emotional-well-being-in-children/

Child Mind Institute. (n.d.). *10 tips to help dads and daughters stay close*. https://childmind.org/article/10-tips-help-dads-daughters-stay-close/

Deneault, A.-A., Bakermans-Kranenburg, M. J., Groh, A. M., Fearon, P. R. M., & Madigan, S. (2023). Child-father attachment in early childhood and behavior problems: A meta-analysis. *Psychological Bulletin*. https://doi.org/10.1037/bul0000383

End Sexual Violence CT. (n.d.). *8 ways to teach kids about consent and healthy boundaries*. https://endsexualviolencect.org/8-ways-to-teach-kids-about-consent-and-healthy-boundaries/

Family Institute at Northwestern University. (n.d.). *Modeling vulnerability*. https://www.family-institute.org/behavioral-health-resources/talking-kids-you-love/modeling-vulnerability

Focus on the Family. (n.d.). *13 lessons dads can teach their daughters*. https://www.focusonthefamily.com/parenting/13-lessons-dads-can-teach-their-daughters/

Focus on the Family. (n.d.). *Dads and the influence they have on their daughters*. https://www.focusonthefamily.com/family-qa/dads-and-the-influence-they-have-on-their-daughters/

Focus on the Family. (n.d.). *How to talk to your daughter about puberty*. https://www.focusonthefamily.com/parenting/your-daughter-and-puberty/

Gottman Institute. (n.d.). *Rituals of connection: The antidote to big emotions and challenging behaviors*. https://www.gottman.com/blog/rituals-of-connection-the-antidote-to-big-emotions-and-challenging-behaviors/

Grohol, J. M. (2013, July). Fathers, daughters & learning self-esteem. *Psych Central*. https://psychcentral.com/blog/fathers-daughters-learning-self-esteem

Hand in Hand Parenting. (2017, November). *Relational trauma, neuroplasticity, and tools for parents*. https://www.handinhandparenting.org/2017/11/relational-trauma-neuroplasticity-tools-parents/

Harvard T.H. Chan School of Public Health. (n.d.). *Exploring the effect of social media on teen girls' mental health*. https://hsph.harvard.edu/news/exploring-the-effect-of-social-media-on-teen-girls-mental-health/

HealthyChildren.org. (n.d.). *Celebrating heritage: Tips for parents*. https://www.healthychildren.org/English/family-life/family-dynamics/Pages/celebrating-heritage-tips-for-parents.aspx

HelpGuide.org. (n.d.). *Co-parenting and joint custody tips for divorced parents*. https://www.helpguide.org/family/parenting/co-parenting-tips-for-divorced-parents

Langlois, C. (2014, January 5). Fathers, daughters & learning self-esteem. *Psych Central.* https://psychcentral.com/blog/fathers-daughters-learning-self-esteem

Legacy Fathers. (n.d.). *Home.* https://www.legacyfathers.org/

Nielsen, L. (2012). *Father–daughter relationships: Contemporary research and issues.* Routledge.

Nielsen, L. (n.d.). *Father–daughter relationships.* https://nielsen.sites.wfu.edu/fathers-and-daughters/research-book/

Psychological Science. (n.d.). *Effective apologies include six elements.* https://www.psychologicalscience.org/news/minds-business/effective-apologies-include-six-elements.html

Ryan, Ryan & Viglione Family Law. (2021, November). *3 ways co-parents can ensure consistency between households.* https://www.ryanryanfamilylaw.com/blog/2021/11/3-ways-co-parents-can-ensure-consistency-between-households/

Sağkal, A. S., Özdemir, Y., & Koruklu, N. (2019). Direct and indirect effects of father–daughter relationship on adolescent girls' psychological outcomes: The role of basic psychological need satisfaction. *Journal of Adolescence, 74,* 259–267. https://doi.org/10.1016/j.adolescence.2019.06.014

Z Girls. (n.d.). *The power of positive affirmations for teen girls.* https://zgirls.org/resources/power-of-self-affirmations-adolescent-girls

Zero to Three. (n.d.). *The daddy factor: How fathers support development.* https://www.zerotothree.org/resource/the-daddy-factor-how-fathers-support-development/

Printed in Dunstable, United Kingdom